ANCIENT WISDOM

THE MONK WITH NO PAST
2nd Edition

By Paolo Marrone

Translation from the Italian by
Lori Hetherington

Originally published in Italian as *Il Monaco Che Non Aveva Un Passato*

Copyright © 2016 by Paolo Marrone

Translation Copyright © 2017 by Lori Hetherington

All rights reserved.

No part of this book may be reproduced in any form or by any electronic or mechanical means including information storage and retrieval systems, without permission in writing from the author. The only exception is by a reviewer, who may quote short excerpts in a review.

This book is a work of fiction. Names, characters, places, and incidents either are products of the author's imagination or are used fictitiously. Any resemblance to actual persons, living or dead, or locales is entirely coincidental.

Independently published

First Printing: April 2017

2nd Edition: January 2020

Cover image @f9photos

INDEX

THE JOURNEY	1
THE SECRET TO HAPPINESS	21
LISTEN TO THE SOUND OF THE WIND	41
DO NOT REGRET THE BOOKS YOU WILL NEVER READ	63
THE RIGHT BOOK AT THE RIGHT TIME	85
THE REAWAKENING	103
APPENDIX: AUTHOR'S INSIGHTS	121

Dedicated to the tireless who search for truth.

THE JOURNEY

"Travel is a sort of door through which one exits reality into an unexplored world that seems like a dream."
- Guy de Maupassant

I had dreamt of visiting New York for years. I have always loved travelling and on earlier trips across the Atlantic I'd visited a number of cities, such as Los Angeles, Miami, and Tampa but, apart from a short layover once at JFK, New York was still on my list. The States hold special fascination in the hearts of Italians and to visit America is a collective dream.

That summer I decided to treat myself to the Big Apple, the city that never sleeps. I couldn't wait to lose myself among the streets of Manhattan, go shopping, admire the majesty of the Empire State Building, have dinner in a typical restaurant with a view of the Brooklyn Bridge.

It would be a solo trip. I had recently come out of a long-term relationship—we'd lived together for ten years—and I'd spent the last three months trying to put the pieces of my life back together. Now, all I wanted was to lose myself in a trip that would help me clear my mind, a sort of reset. I wanted to start a new chapter in my life with renewed enthusiasm. I needed a new outlook, and surely the distance from the places I knew would offer the detachment I needed to see it all from a fresh perspective.

About four or five years before I had begun reading New Thought authors such as Napoleon Hill, Charles F. Haanel, and Thomas Troward. I read pretty much whatever works of theirs I could get my hands on and thanks to them I came to understand that each person is responsible for their own reality. The idea that I could have the power to determine my own destiny via thought was exhilarating but according to the theories I'd read, influence on reality is exerted on an unconscious level. In other words, totally outside our direct control—a thought that instilled in me considerable terror.

I had begun to realize that for a strange law of the universe, the people in our lives represent a reflection of some aspect of ourselves. So if a person changes on the inside, their external world must also change. In fact, I was fully aware that I was the cause of my recent separation, a response to some internal transformation that had taken place. Understanding this, however, didn't give me comfort. A break-up is always a painful experience and I knew there was still, unfortunately, more to endure.

Pondering the end of my relationship, I suspected that the path of personal and spiritual growth I'd undertaken had been the cause of it all. If that was the case, I was probably, in some way, demolishing my old world to make room for something different that would reflect the new me.

Even if I understood instinctively that things would eventually work out, it was little consolation. I would have preferred to have my subconscious ask my opinion before making a mess of my life in such a drastic way! Indeed it was the sensation of not having control that unnerved me and, I must admit, made me more than a little afraid.

A two-week trip seemed like an opportunity for some precious reflection. I could reorder my past—or at least try to—and start down a new road, renewed and without anchors or emotional restraints.

The day before my departure I scanned the list I'd prepared. Everything was packed, with the exception of a few toiletries I'd put in my bag in the morning. I double-checked to make sure I had my tape recorder, the kind that fits in your pocket, to take audio notes during the trip. I don't like writing much and so it would be a more practical and quicker way to record my thoughts and impressions. I could hardly believe only one night separated me from New York! I couldn't wait to leave.

***

A ray of sunlight bored through a crack in the shutters, striking me in the face and lifting me from my deep sleep. I opened my eyes with effort and looked at the clock on the bedside table, maybe I could doze for a few more minutes before getting up... Shit! It was 9:25! Why hadn't the alarm hadn't gone off?

Frantically, I checked the other clocks in the house but they all confirmed the bitter, dramatically clear truth. I was going to miss my plane. I threw my clothes on all the same and stuffed the last few things into my bag. Maybe there was a chance of catching another flight. I have no idea how long it took me to drive to the airport, but I'm sure I beat all the records.

I dashed through the airport looking for the airline ticket office and, when I finally found it, burst through the door, out of breath. Without considering if it was my turn or not, I blurted out my problem to the first employee I saw.

After a quick check on the computer, the young woman told me the unpleasant truth, "Sir, I'm sorry, but the type of ticket you have doesn't allow you to change your flight." It was true—I'd bought a last minute, super discounted ticket. With a sinking feeling, I realized I'd probably have to fork over a frightening sum if I wanted to take another flight to the same destination.

"Excuse me, but isn't there some way to get on another flight, maybe paying a small penalty?" I asked, or rather begged with my saddest eyes, in hopes of some compassion. Perhaps I could awaken a latent maternal instinct in the heart of the employee across the counter.

"I'm sorry, sir, but as I've already explained, your ticket can't be converted or refunded, and the computer is programmed to block any changes with this kind of fare. The only solution, if you want to go to New York, is to buy a new ticket."

I didn't dare think about how much it would cost. In these situations, you're the one in difficulty—in other words the weak party—and the other guy will stick you with every last cent he can. It was the height of the summer season and for a flight of that type, a ticket could easily cost over a thousand Euros. The word 'discount' is unimaginable in these cases.

I tried to insist, explaining that I couldn't give up on my trip. My vacation dates were fixed, I couldn't change them. The employee's reply, delivered with a smile and the utmost kindness, was however the same.

Resigned and about to put my credit card on the counter, giving her permission to bleed me nearly dry, I heard a very kind voice with a hint of foreign accent say behind me, "If you'd like, perhaps I have a solution to your problem." I turned to face a very distinct gentleman, around sixty, with Asian features, who had obviously witnessed the entire scene.

"You see," he continued, "I have a ticket for Tibet, my homeland, where my wife and I were supposed to stay in a monastery for a week. But unfortunately she fell and broke her leg a few days ago and so we can't leave. I've requested a reimbursement but they've just informed me it's not possible so close to the departure date. However, they will allow me to change the name on the ticket. I know it would be a very different sort of vacation—Tibet is not America—but if you want to have a truly new experience, I'd be happy to give you the entire package, including the stay at the monastery."

He paused, his eyes fixed on mine, perhaps to understand if I was taking his offer seriously. My confusion must have been evident from the stunned expression on my face because he quickly added, "You don't have to pay me for it. I prefer to offer this opportunity to someone else rather than waste it. And for some reason, you seem like just the right person. My wife and I would be pleased if you accept."

Tibet? Stay in a monastery? I was about to politely refuse the offer when something held me back. I remembered reading an article that said there's no such thing as chance: events always, and in any case, happen for some valid reason, even if at the time you can't see it.

A series of apparently random episodes *had* brought me to the situation I was in: my alarm clock had never given me problems before; I met a total stranger who offered me a ticket for a trip to Tibet, including accommodations; not to mention the man's poor wife who broke her leg just before their departure. Come to think of it, a few months before while watching a documentary, I had expressed a desire to visit Tibet someday. But I could never have imagined that the universe would take me for my word and wreak such havoc in order to force me on a trip which, in all honesty, I wasn't even sure I wanted to take.

A little voice inside urged me to accept the offer—it was the only sensible thing I could do in that moment. And not because it was free, or not *only*. I had the sensation that it was useless to fight against the force of fate that, as it appeared, wanted to take me at all costs to Tibet. I shivered at the thought of what other adversities I would have to face if I insisted on going to New York. So, I accepted the gentleman's proposal and thanked him for his generous offer. New York could wait.

The flight was scheduled to leave in seven days—just enough time to request a visa to enter China. It would be a week-long trip, rather than two in New York, but it didn't matter. Evidently this also was part of Destiny's plan for me. Thinking about it, two whole weeks of austere monastic life would be too much for a hopelessly lazy, stuck-in-his-ways citizen of the western world.

While we waited to change the name on the travel documents, the gentleman explained that the trip included a week in close contact with one of the oldest and wisest monks in the monastery. His teachings were based on ancient knowledge handed down through the centuries from one monastery to another, normally revealed only to a small circle of chosen monks. These teachings, he assured, would lead me on the path to understanding the true nature of my being. He also told me that I didn't need to worry about the language. Many years ago some of the monks, and among them my soon-to-be teacher, had studied western languages, so I would be able to communicate with him in English without any problems.

I listened, fascinated, but was also a bit doubtful. I couldn't understand why such reserved teaching would be revealed with such ease to the first foreign tourist who happened to land in those parts. However, it seemed impolite to contradict him so I nodded, pretending to believe what he said without any reserve. Knowing that I would have a chance to rest was more than enough for me, and certainly it would be more than if I'd gone to New York. Besides, I would have a chance to dedicate some time to my person reflections. Wasn't that what I'd wanted?

When the paperwork was complete, I held out my hand to thank him and to take my leave. He took my hand and clasped it with great energy, gazing seriously into my eyes, and said he needed to communicate some very important information to me about the trip. "Can we go somewhere to speak privately?" he asked, all the while gripping my hand.

I must say I was surprised, and even a little worried for his sudden gesture but felt in some way in his debt. "There's a coffee bar across the concourse," I suggested. He didn't really seem dangerous and, in any case, we were in a crowded airport.

As soon as we sat down, without giving me a chance to ask him anything, he said, "An ancient prophecy exists, the origin of which has been lost over time. It says an era will arrive during which the ancient knowledge held in Tibetan monasteries will be divulged to all the Western world, with the aim of facilitating a path toward humanity's awakening.

"According to the prophecy," he continued, "a powerful foreign army will invade Tibet, causing massive devastation among its monasteries and thousands of monks to flee. That will be the signal, without any doubt, of the beginning of this process to divulge the knowledge. It was thus that, several years after the invasion of Tibet by the Chinese army, my wife and I were among the first to be chosen, along with a select group of others, to frequent the monasteries where the knowledge was conserved that had been saved from devastation. For the past twenty years we have gone to Tibet periodically to receive teachings from an old monk who possesses the ancient knowledge. No one knows about the true purpose of our trips—in the eyes of the authorities we are simply travelers who like taking vacation in my homeland."

I couldn't believe my ears but continued to listen without interrupting.

"Those who are ready to receive the teachings," he said, "are chosen and 'called' in ways that, for an uninitiated person, seem random. Coincidences occur, or unexpected or fortuitous events of all sorts, so that the chosen ones come into contact with those who must hand down their teaching. That is how it happened for us. Why we were chosen I don't know, but I can imagine that it had to do with my origins and knowledge of the Tibetan language. At the time, in fact, none of the monks were able to speak anything else. However, no one knows with any certainty why they are chosen. All we know is that behind all this there is a precise and inscrutable divine plan by which the ancient prophecy is being carried out with infallible punctuality and precision."

While the story was fascinating, it neared the incredible. Knowledge that would facilitate the path to a human awakening? And for God's sake, why me? On what basis had I been chosen to carry out such a great and difficult task? For a moment I thought that maybe it was better to buy that ticket for New York after all, before it was too late. But then, remembering everything that had happened that morning, my skepticism slowly gave way to growing interest for what my ears were hearing. If the man was not crazy, the connection between all the morning's strange coincidences had brought me to where I was in that moment and suddenly found a plausible explanation. Perhaps an unacceptable explanation for a rational mind like mine, but seemingly the only one able to put each piece of the intricate puzzle in its place.

Besides, the man didn't seem out of touch with reality at all. If anything, I felt there was something profoundly true in what he was telling me. One of the things I noticed while I listened to his words, in fact, was an immense sense of serenity and deep calm that filtered through his slow, tranquil speech. I had the sensation that he was completely detached from what was occurring around him, as if he were living in a calm sea that was all his. At a certain point, it felt as if his serenity had infected me too. The agitation of the morning, which had been boiling inside me until a few minutes before, simply disappeared. I no longer cared about having missed my flight to New York and, the truly incredible thing, I was overtaken by the sensation of being the one who really wanted that trip to Tibet.

"My wife's accident," the man said, "is a clear signal that our time has come to a close, and it's time to pass things on to someone who is younger than we are. As soon as I saw you enter the ticket office I immediately understood that you were the right person. I felt a strong impulse to propose the trip to you, and when I overheard that you'd missed your flight, I no longer had any doubt. I'm convinced you are the chosen one to take my place. Feel honored for this, because you will come to know things that your mind cannot even begin or dare to imagine. Things that will make you a different person and, believe me, will change your life forever."

With these words he stood up, thanked me with a small bow, hands pressed together at chest height, then quickly walked away, leaving me no chance to reply. He took the escalator that led downstairs and, without turning back, disappeared from my line of sight. I ordered a coffee and sat there alone in the airport bar to think about what had just taken place.

The days that separated me from departure flew by. Fortunately, the visa I needed to enter into Chinese territory was approved without any problems or delays and I spent most of the week searching internet for any information, photos or articles I could find on Tibet and its history. In particular, I read everything I could find on Tibetan monasteries and life inside them.

I discovered that the Tibetans, pushed to the limit by the Chinese invasion, were struggling to maintain their cultural and religious traditions and to hand them down, in any way possible, to future generations. The few Buddhist monasteries that had been spared from Chinese reprisals were among the primary sites where these ancient traditions had a chance for survival.

The moment finally came to pack my suitcase. Temperatures on the high Tibetan plain during the summer months were, from what I'd read, rather mild, despite an average elevation of well over 13,000 feet. So, aside from a few heavier pieces of clothing I'd need during the night, when temperatures were more rigid due to the considerable thermal excursion typical of such environments, I didn't have to pack much differently than I had for my intended trip to New York. The night before my flight I set three different alarms to make sure I didn't oversleep this time too.

Two layovers and more than twenty hours later I arrived in Lhasa, the capital of Tibet. At the airport, a man from the travel agency was waiting for me, a sign with my name on it in his hands. We exchanged ritual greetings and he led me outside to where a monk from the monastery was waiting for me. That was when I discovered it would take another three hours in a run-down van to cross the immense valleys of the high plain before I would reach the monastery. Our journey would take us to elevations as high 14,700 feet. I was the only passenger and from the driver's stammered, faltering replies to my questions, it was immediately clear that he was not among the monks who had studied English. I resigned myself to the fact that conversation during the roadtrip would be nearly impossible and sat in silence, admiring the beauty and distinction of the landscape.

The panorama was totally unfamiliar and extraordinary. The roads we travelled crossed through broad valleys surrounded by imposing mountain chains. Everything seemed immense and the sky was a deep, dark blue that struck me—a person used to pale, light blue skies—as almost unreal. Even the sun seemed bigger and brighter, and I figured it had to be due to the elevation. The air was much thinner than what I was used to and it somehow seemed "lighter", I can't find any other word to describe it. In the beginning, I had to take shorter, more rapid breaths to make up for the lack of oxygen, but after a few hours I got used to it, and didn't think anymore about it.

When the van left the main road and turned on to a small unpaved track, I had the impression we were about to reach the monastery. Aside from the fact that nearly three hours had passed, the most important hint was that the road climbed up the mountain on our right. A road so rough, I thought, that it couldn't possibly lead anywhere, if not to a Tibetan monastery perched on the top of a mountain.

For the last fifteen minutes of the trip, despite all the bumps and jostling, I stretched my neck forward, hoping to catch a glimpse of the monastery from one moment to the next as the vehicle rounded the innumerable curves that made up our approach. Finally my wait was rewarded. After a switchback, at the end of the steep, dusty road, the monastery where I would spend my vacation came into view. It was enormous and imposing like a sleeping giant made of stone. It wasn't a single building as I had imagined it, but rather a complex precinct inside which, I discovered, a great number of people lived, each one busy with various tasks.

Monasteries in Tibet are living villages that abound with individuals who take care of every aspect of their community, not only a religious place but a point of social and cultural reference for everyone who lives in the area. If you think about it, especially considering the extreme conditions in terms of isolation and climate, it couldn't be any other way. Creation of social communities around the religious centers was perhaps the only way to guarantee that people's needs were met and not only their spiritual and cultural needs but also, and above all, their material needs.

The village was set into the side of the mountain and, looking at it from below, I could make out the different buildings that clung to the slope, as much as a hundred feet or so above the main, central building. Some buildings seemed embedded in the rock, as if they had literally been carved out of the cliff face. Taken all together, it was awe-inspiring and dominated the colossal majesty of the great valley embraced by the mountains.

The van pulled up to the main gate and a swarm of young monks—a sea of shaved heads and saffron-colored robes—quickly surrounded the vehicle. I climbed out. A crisp wind gusted, snapping the multi-colored prayer flags strung up between buildings and on poles; the air felt transparent, pristine. In my moment of distraction, one of the monks picked up my suitcase before I could get my hand on it and, with broad smiles, bows and cheerful laughter, the group led me festively toward the entrance. In all my trips, I had never received such a warm welcome.

I made my way into the great building that dominated the entire settlement and found myself in an enormous hall with a very high ceiling supported by long, colorfully painted columns. Adding to the beauty, long red drapery hung down from above. The walls were completely covered with sacred images painted on a background of green hills and flowery meadows. An enormous statue of Buddha sat at the end of the room, surrounded by dozens of candles and incense. Surely the altar, I thought, and the room in which I stood the primary place of prayer in the monastery. I tried to take in all the things there were to admire and, standing in the middle of the room, felt my mouth literally hang open in awe.

At a certain point I heard a voice, with proper English pronunciation, say, "Welcome to our monastery. I hope you had a good trip." I turned and saw a monk smiling at me, waiting for my reply. Overwhelmed by the wonders of the place, I had not heard him walk up.

"Yes, it was fine. Thank you for such a cordial welcome," I replied, smiling back. Finally someone who spoke English! Until then, with the exception of the person at the airport, I hadn't been able to exchange more than two words with any of the local people so being able to speak with the monk was a relief. He explained that it was his task to welcome new initiates and that he knew the couple who'd given me their place very well. He commented on the wife's unfortunate accident but when I tried to discuss with him the incredible circumstances that had brought us together, he interrupted with a laconic, "That which must happen, always happens." I had the impression that the facts I was trying to tell him, which seemed bizarre to me, didn't impress him at all and that he'd commented out of politeness, an utterance to mask his totally different vision of events.

"You must be very tired," he said. "I'll show you to your room. You can have dinner there and find good, restorative sleep so you may be ready tomorrow morning to meet the master." He was right, I was really tired, if not totally exhausted, and greatly appreciated the courtesy of being allowed to rest and stay alone for a while. I had no desire in that moment to meet or talk with anyone, not even His Excellency the Great Master in person.

My room was located in another wing of the building, on an upper floor, accessible by a series of steep stone staircases. The small wooden door was identical to many, many others lining a long corridor. This was clearly one of the monastery dormitories. The room was small with a miniscule window up high on the wall above the bed. A simple niche on the right wall was where I could put my things, and a chair and small wooden table, on the left, completed the furnishings. There was nothing more. He told me I could find the shared bathroom at the end of the corridor, the last door on the left. For the first time since I'd left my own country, I was truly sorry to have not purchased a new ticket to go to New York. But now I was there, in Tibet, and it was useless to regret the past.

When we entered the room the monk asked me kindly to give him my watch and any other clocks I had, as well as my cell phone. Cell phones were of no use in that part of the world and I would have no need for a clock. I wasn't thrilled about turning over my beloved objects but I didn't complain. It was useless to protest, seeing as how I was the one who had chosen to make the trip, I reminded myself. At least that's what I wanted to believe.

Before leaving, he told me with a simple smile that I would be awakened the following morning at precisely five a.m. and that someone would bring my dinner soon. Indeed, a few minutes later two young monks entered: the first carrying my suitcase and the other a wooden bowl containing my dinner. They bowed to me deeply, repeatedly, and I mimicked their movements, moving my head in unison with theirs until they left.

I sat on the edge of the bed in that tiny cell in a Tibetan monastery perched on a mountain in the Himalayas, with no idea of how many thousands of feet above sea level I was, nor how many hundreds of miles there were to the nearest town. It was one thing to see photos on internet and completely another to be forlorn and lonely in a foreign country. How long would I resist before running away to catch the first flight back to the life I knew in Italy?

THE SECRET TO HAPPINESS

Real generosity toward the future consists in giving everything to the present.

-Albert Camus

I wondered, before I fell asleep, how they would wake me in the morning.

My curiosity was duly satisfied. At dawn, I heard an insistent, metallic tinkling. At first I heard the sound coming from the end of the hall and with each passing second it grew louder. I assumed it was a monk with bronze cymbals looped on his fingers, walking along the corridor, rousing everyone in the dormitory. Whoever it was, it was effective. In a matter of seconds I was fully awake.

I sat up, stretched, and looked around. A maroon robe, the type that the young monks at the monastery wore, was folded on the chair next to me with a note on top: "Please wear." No telling how the garment got there; I would have surely heard someone enter my room during the night, wouldn't I?

I washed up and shaved in the communal bathroom at the end of the corridor, went back to my room, and tried to figure out how to wear the robe. It might seem easy, but if you've never done it before, it's hard to tell which is the front and which is the back. With a bit of intuition, a considerable dose of good luck, and several clumsy attempts, I finally succeeded in putting it on. More or less. I found a small pocket at chest height and I slipped my small tape recorder into it. It was the only object from Western civilization I'd been allowed to keep.

So, my first full day of vacation—if you can call it that—began. I was anxious to meet the master and finally receive his precious teachings. That was why I had travelled to this lost corner of the world, wasn't it? I held tightly onto this thought as I inexpertly lifted the hem of my robe with each step of the steep staircase. I think I was trying to convince myself that I couldn't run away, at least not until I'd met my mentor and discovered what incredible secrets he had to reveal to me.

Entering the great room, I was struck by the intense smell of incense. Then I noticed about ten monks grouped in a circle on dark red cushions around a multicolored carpet. In the center of them sat a large teapot with steam escaping from its spout. I recognized the monk who had welcomed me and showed me to my room the day before. There was also an elderly monk, the only one amongst them with a long white beard, sitting on a larger cushion. My intuition told me he was the master whom everyone had spoken to me about. Each monk's attention was directed toward him—he was clearly the center of gravity of the group. I could feel his great authority in the air and how it was recognized without reserve by all the monks present.

I tried to guess how old he was but didn't come to a firm conclusion. His mottled, wrinkled skin suggested he was old, but this was contrasted by the vitality and energy that emanated strongly from his gaze. Maybe over ninety, I said to myself, but looking carefully at his eyes it suddenly didn't matter.

The monks sitting closest to the master spoke with him and nodded their heads while the others watched and listened as they sipped what was perhaps tea from big, colorful ceramic cups. Everyone smiled and expressed tranquility, just like the elderly gentleman who had offered me the trip. I took hesitant steps toward the group, hoping someone would notice me and give me a sign of how to behave. I tried to listen to what the monks were saying but their language was totally incomprehensible. I felt like an intruder, light years away from the world around me, a world I knew nothing about and could never belong to.

Suddenly, all the monks stood up, pressed their hands together and bowed slightly toward the master and walked quickly away with small steps. I stood there, immobile, little more than an arm's length away from the now-empty cushions. I hadn't expected to remain alone with him and would have given anything to call the monks back, to beg them to stay there with us. What was I supposed to do? My embarrassment, however, was alleviated when he lifted his eyes and, with a broad smile, gestured for me to take a seat on the cushion closest to him.

I sat down rather awkwardly, my arms and legs caught up in the long robe. I wasn't used to all those folds of fabric and once I settled on the cushion I carefully covered the lower part of my body so that nothing was left exposed. Not knowing if I was supposed to be the first one to speak I tried a timid, "Good morning, master."

He didn't respond and remained perfectly still, his eyes closed. Maybe he hadn't heard me, and I wondered if I should greet him again more loudly, if for nothing else than to break the dramatic silence. Not wanting to make a mistake, I opted to sit quietly and, since I'd finally found a comfortable position, observe him and wait.

Resting with his eyes closed and a hint of a smile, the master finally broke the silence.

I sense that your mind is troubled. You are captive of a thousand questions about why you are here, how you should behave, and what you should do to gain my favor. Your mind is not at peace as you try to imagine how others might see you. You are at the mercy of an illusory world and you try to protect yourself from it with frenetic mental activity, formulating hypotheses about what others think.

The more you agitate, the more the imaginary cords that bind you constrict. You are like a little bird caught in a hunter's net. It flutters and struggles to free itself, but its thrashing does nothing more than tighten the net that holds it prisoner. However you are unaware that you are both the hunter and the little bird, and you fight against yourself uselessly in hopes of dealing with a situation that you, yourself, have created.

I was shocked by his words. It seemed he could read my mind. He'd expressed my sensations better than I could have explained them myself. It was true, I was obsessed by what the master and the other monks thought of me. I was clumsy in that robe and I was sure they could see how embarrassed I was, thoughts that had been gnawing at my mind from the moment I set foot in the room.

Finally, his eyes fluttered and he came out of the trance that had apparently allowed him to look inside me. He lifted his face and smiled.

Relax. Every time you worry about what others think, you become their prisoner. Your mind creates the situation and then it begins to fight against it in order to get away. It is only after having understood that no problem exists—other than the one in your mind—that you can free yourself of it. This is always true. Even when you believe there is no way to escape. You have the ability to make your problems disappear at any moment simply by understanding their illusory nature and, above all, by realizing you are their only creator.

"I beg your pardon, master," I said, "but this is all completely new for me and..."

He interrupted me before I could say anything more.

You needn't apologize. That which you believe to experience is made of nothing. Your excuses demonstrate that you are still bound by the illusory situation created by your mind. Lower your defenses, step out of the illusion. Your ears hear my words, but your mind refuses to understand their meaning.

At this point he stopped speaking and closed his eyes again, pulling his bushy white eyebrows down low as if he were concentrating on my thoughts.

Calm your mind and reconnect with the center of your being. This is the way to understand my teachings. Now, close your eyes and follow my instructions. Concentrate all your attention on your breathing..."

I tried to stay as still as possible and do as he said but my breath was tense and shallow. It's amazing, when you take the time to notice, just how honestly your body reflects how you feel. In that moment, I felt nervous and out of my element and he obviously could tell.

Breathe from your diaphragm, he said, his voice soft and low. *Make your breathing slower and deeper. Pause briefly after you exhale and before you take your next breath. Observe the interval and feel the vitality that courses through your body. Feel yourself sitting here, in this moment. You are full of life, feel it deeply. Turn all your attention to your being. You are, and need be, nothing more.*

His voice trailed off, leaving me to experiment with what he'd just told me. I sat there—for a minute? for five? I have no idea—with my eyes closed, listening only to my sensations.

Observe your body and your mind with detachment, as if they do not belong to you. Identify yourself with the observer and make no attempt to comprehend your emotions or thoughts. Let everything unfold naturally. You believe you control what occurs within you, but the energy you use to try and control that which is uncontrollable comes back inexorably to work against you. Things occur, period. Your ability to choose lies only in the decision of whether to fight against them or observe them.

Again, the master paused for a long while, I assume to give me time to relax and stop trying to control my mind. And it seemed to be working! My breathing was becoming a little calmer and deeper, and I felt a hint of interior stillness that only a moment before seemed impossible.

You are calmer now. Now you may open your eyes, and you will listen. For most of your life you have resisted your thoughts and emotions and by not paying attention you believed you negated them. However, you have seen how futile it is to try and exert control; placing scarce attention on your reality has kept you from learning from your experiences. You have always obstinately refused to recognize this fact, even though all the evidence indicates that this absurd behavior leads to failure.

This is one of the most important keys to existence and you must always keep it in mind.

His words upset me, and greatly. With one single stroke he brought into question an entire castle of beliefs upon which I had based my existence. Maybe he had a point, although I couldn't help but object. "Master, it's difficult to be impassive when faced with the vicissitudes of life. People experience thoughts and emotions as a result of events and experiences.

It's normal to be sad if something unpleasant occurs, or upset if we find ourselves in an uncomfortable situation."

The master seemed indifferent to my words. He looked me straight in the eye and let what seemed like unending moments of silence pass. I probably shouldn't have interrupted him with my stupid objections, I told myself. I was there to learn, and the deafening silence that became the backdrop to his penetrating gaze was probably intended to remind me of it.

Then, because I think he perceived my discomfort, he reassured me with a loving and serene tone. *I understand it is difficult for you to comprehend my words. I can also understand your distress when I do not immediately respond to your objections. Do not take my pauses as a form of displeasure or a form of judgment. Instead, a pause can help keep the mechanical part of one's being in check.*

You will learn that when the mind identifies with the ego it wants—at all costs—to be right and it behaves in an uncontrolled, compulsive way. Instead, a being that does not identify with the mind has learned to be present and to observe the reactions of the ego, which is driven to respond immediately, forcefully advancing its own reasons. A pause is how a wise man silences the egotistical mind, making it possible to observe his own reactions and not identify with them.

An awakened being can never be forced into a conflict, be it verbal or physical, without granting consent. You will understand the importance of pausing when you learn to be present with yourself, and to observe your mind with detachment.

I had been sitting with the master for only a brief while and already I had received a multitude of teachings. So even the pauses were precious opportunities for learning! This trip was turning out to be a fantastic and unusual experience. I felt grateful.

Now, with regard to your objection, it could seem so in the eyes of someone who does not know how the world truly works. The great error you are making is not understanding that what seems to be the cause is in reality only the effect. You are not sad because something unpleasant has happened, rather something unpleasant happens because you have cultivated the habit of being sad.

Not knowing this important law, you tend to ignore the primary cause of the events in your life. First comes the thought: the only, single cause for that which occurs. Then, observing the result of your creation, you react to it in a mechanical way and end up believing that your emotion is the result of the external event. You have inverted effect with cause but, more than that, you have ignored the true objective of this creation mechanism.

He lifted the index finger of his right hand to underline the importance of what he was about to reveal.

Listen to me carefully. You are on this earth to create your own reality, with the single aim of learning from it. You are the observer who, through the simple act of observing, can decide what you wish to give your attention to. But you are also a divine being and, as such, the universe cannot do anything but respond by seconding your thoughts and materializing, in your reality, whatever you give your attention to. You are at the root of everything. This is a fundamental concept.

It is not possible for you to modify that which you are experiencing in the here and now. Things appear because you ask for them and it is your task to experience them. That which you experience is the result of your previous choices: once they materialize they cannot be modified because they are crystallizations of past thoughts. The reality you experience is like clay shaped by the expert hands of a craftsman. It can be worked into any shape, such as a vase for example, but once it is put in the kiln and fired it can no longer be changed. It would be ludicrous for the craftsman to change the final result of his work with a hammer, he would be left with nothing but a pile of rubble.

In the same way, it is equally ridiculous to oppose the present moment by complaining, judging, or inflaming with anger. Doing so, you give up your power and delegate it to external forces. When you set yourself against the present moment, you are negating your own creation. Instead, demonstrate your wisdom by acting on the true cause: act on your thoughts and understand that what you see is simply the materialization of your previous choices. If you learn to act by modifying that which occurs within you, your reality will then reflect your change in perspective. It is the only way.

You have always been taught that free will is expressed in the freedom to do, when instead it is exclusively the freedom to choose where you place your attention, which thus means the freedom to choose what to experience.

If something does not appeal to you, remove your attention from it and concentrate instead on that which you desire with the aim of experiencing it. This is the free will that is bestowed upon you as a divine being at the time of your birth. It is the only free will that exists in nature and, as such, it is the only one you have the ability to exert.

This truth has always been right before your eyes. Many times you have faced the harmful effects of obtuse resistance toward the things of the here and now that do not satisfy your expectations. And placing your attention on them did nothing but reinforce with the universe your request for those things. As I've told you, the universe can do nothing but obey your will.

You have the ability to choose through mindfulness, and this is how you create the reality you are destined to experience. This is the great, singular truth that your blindness has never allowed you to see.

Did I hear him correctly? It seemed he was saying that free will is nothing more than the freedom to choose one's own thoughts and this choice then translates into subsequent life experiences. If it was true, in a few words he'd presented the most logical and plausible explanation I'd ever heard of the Law of Attraction.

I'd always struggled to understand new concepts but I realized that after the breathing exercise the master taught me I felt as if I could hear his words more clearly. It took me less effort. When I relaxed and observed, I actually felt more in control of myself.

As I listened to the master, a young monk came and poured tea into a cup from the steaming pot then placed it back at the center of the carpet delicately. I thanked him with a nod of my head and received in return a bow and a broad smile. He withdrew facing the master, walking backwards, his hands joined in front of his chest and his head lowered out of respect.

The serene expression on the monk's face reminded me of the joyous welcome I'd received the day before. In fact, I had noticed how everyone I met at the monastery was constantly smiling, including the master who was kind and loving. It seemed as if I had landed in a strange world where sadness was banned and people were happy and untroubled, no matter what. I was curious about the reason for such joy and said, "Master, I've noticed that everyone who lives in the monastery always seems happy, but how can a person be happy for no apparent reason? What's the secret?"

Serenity comes from a deep knowledge of one's intimate nature. His words were unhurried. *If you knew you were eternal, and that nothing your eyes saw could ever bring you harm, wouldn't you be happy to be alive in this earthly experience? If you were aware of the fact that what you are living is only a marvelous dream and that the entire universe is working in your favor so that you may raise your level of awareness, higher and ever higher, moving you closer and closer to your true divine essence, wouldn't you be happy too?*

What was he saying? For millions of people the world is a place of sacrifice and pain, full of war, injustice, and atrocities of all sorts. How could simply understanding one's nature alleviate this suffering and render a person happy, regardless of what was happening around him?

It is normal for you to be confused.

How did he know how I felt? I hadn't said anything.

You will never be able to comprehend my words as long as you continue to believe that happiness must necessarily depend on an external cause. As long as you search for happiness outside of yourself, you will be destined for failure. By waiting for an external cause, you are confounding cause with effect.

Don't you remember? I said that you are at the origin of everything. Other causes outside of yourself do not exist. First create the effect you desire, and then the cause will manifest itself.

"How can I create the effect first? Isn't that backwards? If I really want to have something, how can I create it first?"

You are focusing on the wrong target. First you must fully understand what 'effect' means. Ask yourself what is the purpose of your desire. You do not desire something simply to possess it, you wish to taste the joy of possession. The final effect to which you aspire, therefore, is not possession as a means unto itself but rather the emotion that is generated from it. Your aim is not to possess things, it is to be happy. You erroneously believe that happiness can derive from the possession of some material object and thus lose sight of your true, ultimate objective.

This is the great mistake, and you are one of its victims. For this reason you believe true happiness is unattainable without an apparent cause. The effect you crave is the emotion of joy and it is the only thing you are able to control and upon which you have exclusive and unconditional power. Think of the clay I mentioned before. If you wish, you can shape it into a vase through your emotions, which are under your direct control. Happiness is a choice, and it transcends all material achievement.

Be happy and the world will contrive something to justify your happiness. Create the effect and the cause will manifest itself. This is the secret you asked about. It has always been before your eyes but you have insisted on ignoring it.

"Master, I think I get the part about delighting in the happiness of possessing things but I still don't understand how I can be happy without there first being a reason. Hard as I try, I just can't believe a person can decide 'I'm going to be happy' or 'I'm going to be sad'. Please, help me understand."

The answer is simple and it has always been right before your eyes. You just think you don't know. You reveal your blindness when you say you don't have reason to be happy here and in this moment.

When that disciple poured the tea for you a short time ago, you thanked him and this made you feel good for a brief time. Gratitude is one of the most powerful instruments to induce in our mind a state of blessedness. It sends away illusory thoughts of fear and worry. You thanked him because you received something that you considered pleasant, and that perhaps you had even desired.

Look around at all the things that are available to you, just like the tea. You enjoy excellent health, you have a home, many things that fill your life and that permit you to be happy. If you did not, you would probably desire to have them, convinced that having them would render you happy. You already have those things, so why are you not happy now?

Why did you feel the need to thank the disciple for having poured a simple cup of tea but do not feel the need to thank the universe for all the beautiful things that are already part of your life? This is the path to happiness. Do not wait for something to happen in the future; the future is only an illusion created by your mind. Instead, feel grateful in the here and now for all the things you already possess and that make your life pleasing.

When you wake up, thank the bed for having kept you warm during the night; thank your body for allowing you to live and experience the beauty of life. Remember to express immense gratitude for your home and the food you eat every day. Celebrate everything you already have with joy. This is how you will move closer to the truth, to your true essence, and it will lead you to the light of your happiness.

Remember, you are creating a world in which confirmation of your emotions and sensations is the single aim. I have explained that by exercising your free will you can easily choose where to direct your attention, and thus control what you feel. This means you hold the key to choosing what you experience.

I was about to reply that, although I got the importance of being grateful for the things in life, the connection between gratitude, truth, and happiness wasn't so clear. But as soon as I opened my mouth, the master lifted his hand to halt my words.

You continue to listen to your unsettled mind. It obtusely insists on bringing what I say back to something you know. You cannot grasp with your mind that which does not belong to the kingdom of the intellect.

Listen carefully. Unlike illusion, truth does not require confirmation, it does not need you to believe in its existence. It already is. It has always existed, and it will continue to exist after the last of your illusions have disappeared. Eliminate what is not real and what impedes truth from coming to the surface.

Perhaps it will surprise you, but truth and happiness are exactly the same thing. Or more precisely, happiness is another one of your senses and through it you will understand when you are near truth.

Instead, the deeper you are immersed in illusion, the farther you are from truth and the more you will lack happiness. When your mind is invaded by thoughts of worry or fear, it is as if you are sleeping while your eyes are open. Immersed in your dream, you are far, far from truth. Your dream makes you believe in the existence of a world that does not exist, and this blocks you from ultimate truth. You can only move closer by eliminating the countless layers that, like grey clouds, keep you from experiencing light and warmth.

When you appreciate something, and as a consequence are grateful, you eliminate some of those barriers. Gratitude frees your mind from noise and leads you closer to truth. And when you are closer to truth you feel better because you are beginning to glimpse true reality which, like sunshine on a cold day, gives you relief. That relief is what you perceive as happiness. It is always present beyond your miserable thoughts, exactly like the warm rays of the sun are always present beyond the layer of clouds.

Happiness is always present... truly a disconcerting concept. But then it dawned on me that maybe the restlessness that had been dwelling in me came from the mental noise and, as the master had just explained, it was keeping me from truth and resulting happiness. I had to eliminate the layers that were in the way so I could move closer. Maybe it was true that I had been making my life difficult with absurd, useless mental rumination. Maybe happiness truly was at hand and I just had to want it. Well, that explained why everyone seemed so happy. They'd eliminated the obstacles that kept them from what the master called truth.

I had to ask him—I couldn't go on any longer without knowing. "Master," I said, "I think I'm beginning to understand how appreciation and gratitude can help keep my mind free from negative thoughts, which is what keeps me from truth. But what is this truth that you speak of? Where do I find it and how can I recognize it?"

He extended his hand. *Help me stand up and I will show it to you.*

LISTEN TO THE SOUND OF THE WIND

Look at the birds of the air; they neither sow nor reap nor gather into barns, and yet your heavenly Father feeds them. Are you not of more value than they?

-Mathew 6:26

I finally saw the master on his feet. He was not particularly tall—probably only about five foot four—but I felt small in his presence. He exuded authority and greatness and you could feel it, simply standing next to him. His back was erect, despite his advanced age, his head held high and his gaze deep.

His movements struck me as slow, but not due to his age. Instead, they seemed deliberate, the result of meticulous and constant attention to his gestures, to his body and being, and to everything around him. Maybe this too was a demonstration of what living with presence meant, constantly in the here and now. As I write these words, I realize how difficult it is to express what I felt in his presence. The whole experience was wondrous.

He motioned for me to follow him and we approached a small wooden door at the back of the room, facing the mountain and opposite from where people entered the great hall. I couldn't imagine where it led since it seemed the building abutted against the bare rocky cliff.

Before opening the door, he stopped and turned, perhaps to be certain I was with him. Then he opened the door, and we crossed the threshold.

I couldn't believe my eyes. In front of me was a beautiful garden, tucked into a nook in the mountain behind the main building of the monastery. The ground was covered by a well-tended layer of bright, thick green grass. Tiny, colorful flowers dotted the expanse of lawn, offering places to alight for the dozens of carefree, small white butterflies that flitted about. Dense vegetation climbed up the cliff in front of us and a small waterfall, probably formed from rainwater that collected along the mountain face, splashed and gurgled. Once the cascade reached the bottom of the drop, it fed a stream that crossed the garden for its entire length and the water, channeled in this way, eventually flowed into a small pond on my left. Large lotus leaves floated imperturbably on its surface.

A true spectacle of nature, totally hidden to the indiscreet eyes of occasional visitors. I'm sure no one would ever imagine that something so beautiful could hide behind an unassuming wooden door in the most remote and darkest corner of that enormous room. I obviously didn't.

"Oh, I had no idea..." I muttered.

That is precisely your problem. You assume things that are not true. Your entire life is based on assumptions that, upon trivial verification, are revealed as completely without foundation. In this particular case it would have been sufficient to wait and see what was on the other side of the door. Instead you employed your mind to formulate a hypothesis. I could tell, simply by looking at your face before I opened the door. With a glance I could see the doubt that clenched your mind, fruit of a thousand assumptions that without reason and in a totally arbitrary way you adopted in that moment. When the door swung open, your hypothesis was revealed to be incorrect.

You live in an illusory world and you believe that many things in it are certain, but you do not notice that none of them are true. These beliefs are really illusions that, for the most part, you have acquired from others and then blindly accepted them to be so. You accept that the world you see is concrete and that it continues to exist also without you.

You assume nothing can happen without a previous cause, and therefore you do not believe in the possibility of being happy regardless. This belief strongly limits all aspects of your life. You do not realize that you constantly live in a world where your experiences correspond to your most intimate beliefs. With your conviction that gratifying, unexpected events are impossible, you render your life monotonous and flat.

He was absolutely right. I had assumed that nothing interesting could exist behind the door.

The master kept figuring out my most intimate feelings and thoughts, as if I could hide nothing from him. I have to admit, it made me feel uncomfortable. How did he do it? Maybe I gave myself away with my facial expression, or maybe he possessed sensory skills that were different from those of us common mortals. Whatever the reason, I felt naked in his presence, and I'm sure he was aware of it. More than once that morning, I noticed him trying to attenuate my distress with a warm smile or conciliatory words in hopes of reducing the great distance that seemed to separate us.

He stood still for several moments then inhaled before continuing.

You have asked me what truth is.

We arrive at it by degrees. The path that leads us to understand what is truth is long and tortuous, and along that way you must demolish many false beliefs about yourself and the world. The first thing you have to know is that truth resides within you. It is part of your being, even if you are convinced it can be found elsewhere, hidden perhaps in a book or in the words of a guru.

Until you understand that you have to look for it inside yourself, you will be destined to search in vain. It is the only place you can find it. There is a marvelous garden inside, even though right now you cannot even imagine it exists. At times you may perceive there is a way to gain access to it but, just as you assumed there was nothing behind a plain wooden door, you disregard it because you believe it is completely insignificant. You can enter your marvelous garden only when, in rare moments, your mind is absolutely quiet. However, you do not notice those moments for what they are and, with misguided conviction, believe that silence leads you nowhere.

If instead you were to stop and observe that silence, you would become aware that the door leads you toward truth and your true self. Everything else is just mental noise, and as such it has no real consistency. That is what creates the illusion you are constantly immersed in—your believing it is reality.

"So," I began tentatively, "if I understand correctly, truth needs to be encouraged to emerge, to be brought into the light. A person has to recognize it and bring it to the surface, not leave it trapped under illusion. Is that right?" I could barely contain my pride at perhaps having understood what his words really meant.

You can neither force nor bring to the light that which, in reality, is already light. The sun is not linked in the slightest to the alternating of day and night on Earth. Its light exists regardless. The sun knows that darkness does not exist as an entity in and of itself. It can only be conceived as an absence of light, as something that can be described only in function of its primary cause, which is light itself. You cannot become a merchant of darkness: how could you sell something that does not exist?

Once again the master must have read in my eyes how I was struggling to follow his reasoning.

I understand this is difficult to understand. But once you have grasped why that which is not real is devoid of consistency, you will find a smooth path toward the answers to your questions.

Illusion, like darkness, cannot live on its own. This is the first precious clue I can offer to help you recognize what is not real. Just as darkness disappears when it is illuminated, illusion dissolves to reveal its ephemeral nature when faced with the light of truth.

"Pardon me, but I feel like I'm back where I started. You say that in order to discover what is not real I have to use the light of truth, but if I don't know what truth is, how can I use it to illuminate what is false?"

Your mind is as eager and impatient as a puppy that wiggles and jumps to get hold of its dish while its master is preparing the food. The puppy does not understand that the contents of the dish will be his no matter what, all he has to do is wait. Just as the food must be prepared before the puppy can eat it, so must your mind be prepared before it can fully understand the meaning of my words.

You will make a true step forward when you understand that illusion needs you in order to exist since it cannot live on its own. It has an absolute need for you to believe it is real, otherwise it is unable to manifest itself. Illusion is kept alive by your belief, which in turn is fed by your lack of awareness. The result is that you are prisoner of a deep, deep slumber through which the light of truth cannot penetrate, but you are unaware of being both prisoner and jailer. You live in a dream, but the dream cannot exist without a dreamer. Now perhaps you are beginning to understand why I say that you are at the root of your world. That world is without consistency although you believe it to be real, and thus it cannot exist without your recreation of it, moment by moment, in the way you believe it should appear.

Recreate the world moment by moment... what did that mean? How can someone recreate something that already exists? I see the world here around me, and although the master had already explained that it originates with me, I didn't get what he meant with the word 'recreate'.

Unexpectedly, concepts of quantum physics came to mind: the so-called 'quantum broth'. According to the theory, which I had studied enthusiastically, an empty space is not actually empty because really it is composed of a bubbling of particles that enter and exit continually. Through observation, we literally 'extract' from the broth only the configurations of particles that make up the objects and events in the world that we see in that instant. Perhaps this was the physical mechanism the master was referring to when he said that the world is recreated moment by moment. Could Eastern doctrines have possessed knowledge of quantum concepts in the most distant of times? Maybe so. I knew that official science had made discoveries in recent decades that offered parallels. So it was natural for me to ask him about it. "Actually, this brings to mind quantum physics," I said. "According to the theory, we can potentially extract anything from any portion of empty space. Is this how we recreate the world?"

He looked up to watch a flock of birds that had just lifted into flight.

The scientists of your world are very far from understanding reality. They believe they observe a pre-

existing world that is separate from them. You cannot explain matter with matter, or energy with energy. Until scientists introduce consciousness into their formulas, they will never grasp the true nature of things. They believe they have discovered a world, but it is what they are creating themselves and they will always find confirmation of their theories in it, even the most extravagant ones. If a sufficient number of scientists believe in a theory, then sooner or later it will be confirmed by an experiment. It is only a question of time.

This truth has always been right before their eyes. Indeed, if you observe the history of scientific discoveries from another point of view, you will find confirmation. Take a formula that hypothesizes the existence of a new law of physics as an example. If it is considered sufficiently reliable by the scientific community and it is mathematically elegant, then you can be certain that the law will find confirmation sooner or later in some experiment. Scientists will not become conscious of this truth, which anyone can see given the right conditions, until they accept that they are the only creators of the world in which they carry out their experiments.

"But master, if that law of physics is discovered it's because it already exists, and therefore it has always existed. I can't believe that it starts being true only because some scientist has hypothesized it. The world you describe is too strange to be credible."

The world you see is the one you are creating and it adapts to your beliefs of how it should appear or behave. The laws of physics are in no way determining. Different from what scientists believe, the universe is nothing more than the constant expression of humanity's level of awareness, manifesting laws that vary in function of what can commonly be accepted as true. Science cannot explain illusion because science, itself, is one of the many manifestations of it. You realize you have been dreaming only when you wake up and look at your reality with different eyes, and this can only occur at a heightened level of awareness. I know that it may seem incredible for someone like you who still thinks that the world is something external that exists regardless of who observes it, but that is precisely what happens. In fact, some scholars from your world are beginning to realize it.

"But the fact remains that a law of physics, in order to be discovered, has to already exist in the universe," I said, although once I'd uttered it I wasn't so sure. The master, up until then, had handily demolished my certainties one at a time.

Again you are confusing cause with effect. There is nothing to discover because nothing can exist if it is not first conceived at a mental level. Through your mind you literally give permission to things to exist and to manifest themselves. This is the case for anything or any event you experience: for scientific progress or an occurrence in your life, whether it is happy of unhappy. You are at the center of your world, and you are the origin of it. When you believe to be separate from your true self, you create a world where duality and separation reign, mere projections of your most intimate beliefs. The problem is that you have forgotten you are the creator of your world, thus you've lost awareness of its illusionism.

"I'm just trying to apply the rules of common sense I've learned throughout my life," I replied timidly. "It's logical to assume that what I see or what I experience must, in some way, already exist." As soon as the words came out of my mouth, I realized it was more a question to myself than a statement, and I wasn't so sure there was an answer to it.

Your ears hear my words but your mind acts as a constant filter, relegating to oblivion everything that does not match with your past experience. I have already said that your greatest problem is assuming what is not, such as the objective existence of the world around you. You try desperately to compare what I say to something you know, but you must embrace the idea that the past cannot help you understand. You will not be able to take a single step toward truth until you stop assuming the existence of a reality independent of your being. Anything—from a law of physics to a material object—cannot exist if it has not previously been conceptualized in your mind. However this is extremely difficult for you to accept because you insist on assuming the existence of an external world. In turn, this leads you to come to the incorrect conclusion that your task is to 'discover' it.

"Master, if I am the one who creates things when they appear and enter into my reality, it means I can experience them, therefore for me they are the truth. They are true because they exist."

Don't be misled by my words. When I say that something 'exists' as a consequence of your thought as creator, I do not mean that it has an actual 'existence': it is and will always be an illusion. Do not confuse experience with what is truth. You are referring to truth as something that is apparently outside of yourself, while you can only find it within. You must keep this constantly in mind during your search.

He looked straight into my eyes and rested his hand on my shoulder.

Listen carefully. I am about to reveal what the world you believe you see is made of.

A sudden gust of wind came up violently and rustled the plants around us. He paused but continued gazing into my eyes while the wind tugged at our long robes. His hand squeezed my flesh, almost as if he wanted to keep me from being swept up by the impetus of the wind.

At the time, I thought the event occurred by chance but now, in hindsight and considering what the master was telling me at that moment, I interpret the gust as a divine whisper of awareness, invoked to sweep away the accumulation of false certainties that cluttered my mind.

Several seconds after the wind died down, the master continued speaking.

You are entangled in a vicious cycle. You believe that you are separate from all that is, and as a consequence you constantly create from nothing a dual world in the image of your erred belief, which is apparently separate from you. At the same time you observe your creation, forgetting that you are its creator, and fall into the illusion that what you see is reality. Your observation reinforces your beliefs, leading you to the illusion that you are right in believing that what you experience truly exists. And so on, further and further in an unending cycle. You have fallen so deeply into the spiral of your illusion that you can no longer perceive even the distant reflection of the place of light from which you came.

Like the cat that puffs its fur and hisses threateningly at its own reflection in a mirror and is then surprised that the cat on the other side of the glass is not frightened at all, you are blinded by a game of light and shadow and are unaware of being the only creator and protagonist. The world you see is only a projection of your self, thus your senseless battle against the world is nothing more than a battle against yourself. Understandably, it is not easy to break free from it. Indeed, until you are ready to recognize the deception, you will call those who try to make you aware of your delirium crazy, and you will fight with all your strength to resist, even though your illusory world scares you to death.

That which is not real hides the truth from you and disguises itself as reality. You have unconditionally believed in this game for all of your lives, without ever questioning yourself. But then a moment comes and you realize something is not right. The world you have always believed in suddenly seems to no longer make sense and you start searching for truth. Naively you believe you can find it somewhere outside of yourself, perhaps in a spiritual leader or in the pages of a book, but looking in the wrong place does nothing more than reinforce your illusion. Truth is not located in a single place. It is the origin of everything and what everything you can experience derives from. It is your task to discover and recognize what is not real, for it is in this way that you move closer to understanding truth.

Truth is the fountainhead of all that can exist. It is unchangeable and eternal. It is the spring from which every single thing—known and unknown—emerges. Eventually you will come to realize that all this searching is nothing more than a trip back toward yourself, toward your true self, which is the origin of everything. You need not search for truth because it has always been available to you. Eliminate those things that keep it hidden from your eyes and you will realize you are truth. For this reason you can never find it because the only logical thing you can do is be it.

"I don't understand, master." I was trying so hard to follow him I could feel my brain working inside my skull. "Now you're telling me I don't have to search for truth... I thought that was my main task. You, yourself, told me that finding truth means also finding happiness, and that this is my ultimate goal."

It is impossible for you to search for truth because you would have no chance of finding it. Finding something assumes that you have been separated from the object you are seeking. You have not been separated from truth: you are truth. It is your most intimate nature. How can you find something you already are? It is like looking for your glasses without realizing they are sitting on your nose. Put your efforts instead into cleaning house with the purpose of eliminating everything that is not true and that obscures the vision of who you are. This is your task.

The illusory world you are creating has no apparent sense, and as such it terrifies you. This is why you are unable to perceive the happiness that is already part of your being. Whatever your problem, it is only the result of a hallucination, created by you as a consequence of feeling separated from the world that surrounds you. The only way you can rediscover who you truly are is to eliminate all the excess that darkens your true being.

He had a point. People live in fear that something unpleasant will happen to them and, in fact, I had often given up on opportunities because I was afraid of facing new challenges. I stayed within my comfort zone, where I felt protected from unforeseen experiences.

"Master, I would like very much to consider my problems as simple hallucinations but I find it so hard to eliminate my fears. The world seems to move independently from my will and, like many people, I am afraid that something can happen unexpectedly, whether I want it to or not."

He gestured for me to be silent and turned his eyes skyward.

Listen to distant leaves as they rustle in the wind. Observe clouds transported by the wind. Contemplate how butterflies flutter their wings. It is the universe that puts things in motion to satisfy your desires. Nothing moves without a purpose. Even when the smallest speck of matter moves, it does so to satisfy your requests. Step out of the idea that your body is limited in space and separate from everything else; start considering the entire universe as your own physical body. Just as your heart beats and each cell in your body strives to keep you alive, each part of the Cosmos—even the most remote—aspires to act for your benefit.

He was trying to explain things to me but I felt even more confused. "I often don't reach my objectives because of impediments that get in the way or because what I set my sights on is particularly difficult. What does the Cosmos have to do with it?"

The Master grinned and shook his head with disagreement.

You are far from truth. You struggle with the absurd conviction that only what you are able to conceive with your rational mind can exist, and this confuses your limits with the limits of the world. You are the one who places those impediments between you and the achievement of your desires. There is nothing and no one out there who can do it in your stead. Furthermore, you have completely shifted the significance of the words 'desire' and 'aim', using them not only in the wrong way, but even believing they have the same meaning.

There is only one aim: to return to your origins to rediscover who you really are. Even though you believe you have aims to satisfy in this life, only a single, final aim truly exists: your definitive awakening. This is what I am referring to when I say that the universe plots to satisfy your aim. You cannot know when, but one day you will attain it. It is impossible to fail. As I have told you, the entire universe is on your side.

Instead, the things that you call desires are practically inexistent and of no importance for the universe. It cannot perceive them because they live in your rational mind, the part of you that constantly lives in the darkness of illusion. For the universe, your true desires are nothing more than your beliefs, translated into your expectations. Your entire being constantly vibrates in accordance with everything you believe is possible and it is that vibration that creates, moment by moment, the world in which you have experiences. Nothing can change in your life if first you do not change your primary beliefs which, through the vibrations they emanate, modify into actual orders that the universe can do nothing but carry out. If you want your desires to become reality, stop projecting them into the future and transform them into what you are now. Base them on your beliefs so that they become one single thing. Be what you want to become. If you do it in the here and now, you will see that the doors you thought were closed will open as if by magic.

Yet, lasting change will not take place until you acquire the awareness of who you really are. You will have to practice with constant and firm will, exposing and recognizing all that is false and that belongs to the great illusion in which you are immersed.

I felt my heart beat faster in my chest, something he'd said struck at my core. "Please master, teach me," I begged as my hands came together over the place I felt quiver inside. "Tell me what I need to do and I will dedicate myself entirely."

You already know what to do. That is, if you have listened carefully to what I have said. Retreat into meditation at least once a day, and after having silenced your mind, while your eyes are still closed, ask yourself who you really are. Insist with this practice, throwing out each idea that comes into your mind. You will be learning to perceive that you are beyond anything your mind is able to conceive. You are beyond the dream because you are the origin of it. Through this exercise, the idea will take root that your true self cannot be conceived or described. It is the origin and thus antecedent to all other things.

I focused all my attention on the master; I didn't want to miss a single word.

After you have done this a number of times, bring silence back to your mind. Open your eyes slowly and look at all the things around you, including your body. Each time your gaze or your mind pauses on a particular object, repeat to yourself, 'What I see is not real but only my creation, something in which I have deeply believed.' Your task is to train your mind so that it recognizes what you perceive with your senses as an illusory object. This will help you rise up along the spiral of illusion, clearing away the clouds that block the light of truth one bit at a time.

This is all for today. Your mind has received sufficient material upon which to reflect. Dedicate your afternoon to rest and meditation. Without practice, my words are nourishment wasted on your superficial mind, simple intellectual curiosities that will die together with your body. You must lay down new beliefs in such a way that knowledge becomes experience. Only with practice is it possible to forge a new being. Now go to your room and meditate. Analyze what you believe you know and ask yourself the right questions in order to bring into discussion each of your current certainties.

If you want to understand truth, you must first demolish everything that is not true. Indeed, what is not true will dissolve in the light of awareness like snow in the sun. Stop making foolish assumptions and subject to doubt—always and in any case—everything you believe you know. Only that which is true resists the test of doubt. All else will be revealed for what it is: nothing, and nothing more. Go, begin your sacred path in search of the happiness that is already within you. It is waiting to be brought back to the light.

He turned and walked away, moving slowly toward the waterfall at the end of that marvelous garden. I went back into the large hall where, in the meantime, various monks had gathered to pray. I sat in a corner to observe them and listen to their chanting. I stayed there until lunchtime, pondering the incredible things the master had told me that morning.

After a frugal meal of rice and fruit I went to my room, where I spent the rest of the day practicing as he had instructed me. When fatigue overtook me, I let myself drift into restorative sleep.

DO NOT REGRET THE BOOKS YOU WILL NEVER READ

> *If you want to know the meaning of existence, you should open a book; hidden there, in the darkest corner of one of the chapters, is a sentence written just for you.*
>
> -Pietro Citati

A distant metallic tinkling pulled me—unwillingly—out of my deep sleep. The sound grew louder and I was thrust back into the reality of that tiny room inside a Tibetan monastery, lost among the peaks of the Himalayas, so early it was still dark.

Even without a clock, I could have bet it was exactly five in the morning. Tibetan monks have a developed sense of punctuality, above all when it comes to their rituals. I thought about the fact that for the monks each activity is experienced as if it is a sacred rite, even with regard to those things we consider the most trivial, like pouring tea or announcing the time to wake up in the morning. I rolled onto my back, adjusted the bedcovers and wondered why. The writings of Eckhart Tolle, G.I. Gurdjieff and others came to mind and how they taught the importance of mental silence.

The reason for the rituality, applied with extreme rigor, suddenly became clear. The monks place maximum attention on everything they do, and this leads them to always be in the here and now, with full control of their own minds. In line with the master's teachings, this was how to turn off mental noise, and move closer to truth, and therefore to happiness. Even if I had read about it uncountable times, the true essence of ritual became clear only in that moment: it's not important *what* you do, but *how* you do it. In other words, what really counts toward reaching interior peace is the depth with which you immerse yourself in daily actions.

My thoughts then drifted to how every faith has its own rituals. No matter what the religion, the devout are trained to be present and live in the here and now through rites, sacraments, rituals, and repeated formulas, even if this meaning has been largely lost, except perhaps in some Eastern doctrines. The purpose, however, is essentially the same.

What a distracted mind, especially at five o'clock in the morning, might find irritating—two bronze discs striking against one another—had instead come to represent a precious opportunity to think about the true meaning of the rituals and the importance of being present. Even if I read entire volumes on the topic, I couldn't have gotten the same clarity of understanding that the sound, that morning, was offering me.

I was becoming aware that every situation in the monastery, not just the master's teachings, provided me with the chance to learn something if I held onto the right key. With this exhilarating thought, I swung my legs off the mattress and onto the stone floor and got ready for the long day that awaited me.

One of the monks told me the master would wait for me in the library, in the most westerly part of the complex. To get there, I followed an outdoor path and admired the immense valley that rested at the foot of the mountain. Shiny from the passage of who knew how many pairs of sandals through the centuries, the perfect polish on the large, smooth stones attested to the ancient history of the place. The brisk morning air heightened my senses and every feature of the majestic view stood out in sharp detail. I was filled with a great sense of excitement and expectant joy as I proceeded toward the enormous door at the end of the path.

The doorway to the library was grand—perhaps more than fifteen feet high—and the antique wooden doors were carved with hundreds, probably thousands of tiny figures and ideograms. I had no idea of their significance since my knowledge of oriental art was very limited, but felt certain that such a magnificent door could only lead to a library of inestimable value and immense sacred importance. The beauty of the portal captured my attention and I paused, breathless, like I imagine a person does when viewing over the rim of the Grand Canyon for the first time.

Later I discovered that the moment of contemplation in front of such greatness is the means through which you obtain a momentary suspension of thought, a sort of instantaneous cleansing of the mind, and it's willfully induced to bring visitors to the correct state of mind, to prepare them to enter a venerable place. I can only guess that imposing cathedrals of extraordinary beauty were built in the past, in part, to leave whoever crossed the threshold in awe.

I entered the dim library timidly, searching with my eyes for the master. Finally, after struggling to detect recognizable shapes in the darkness, I heard his clear voice.

Come in. You must learn to not rely so greatly on your eyes. They do not see reality. You are convinced you cannot see me in a place that lacks light, but if you stopped your mind and listened with your senses, you would know immediately where to find me.

Now I knew where to go, but not because I had acquired some extra-sensory skill. It was the direction of his voice that led me. I turned to my right and advanced slowly. After some steps, I was able to make out what looked like a human form at a large table surrounded by books. As I approached, his shape and the many volumes piled around him became clearer thanks to the weak illumination from a small window high up on the wall.

He indicated a bench in front of him, on the opposite side of the heavy wooden table.

Come, sit. You should feel honored. Few disciples before you have had the privilege of crossing the threshold of this place.

"Why is that?" I asked with surprise, as I pulled the silky-smooth plank of wood away just enough to sit down. "Are the monks from the monastery forbidden from entering the library?"

I did not say monks, I said disciples. And you are less than a disciple since you still believe in the existence of a real world outside yourself. A disciple is one who faces the doctrine with a child's curiosity, free from preconception or previous knowledge. A disciple still has a past but understands he cannot base himself on it if he wishes to comprehend the reality of the world that surrounds him.

He paused in a way I was beginning to recognize.

You entered here bringing with you all of your world, which is composed of your past, or what you believe is your past. It is ballast, dead weight that pulls down on your mind and darkens it just enough to impede you from collecting the signals that arrive from your keenest senses, the ones you do not even suspect to have.

I had barely taken my seat and an avalanche of notions was crashing over me. I strained to order them in my mind but questions piled up, creating an obstruction that kept my voice from coming out.

This room is not dark. The darkness you believe to see is only a projection of the darkness that is inside of you. The world could be a bright place, even on a moonless night, but the light has to shine from the inside before it can be perceived on the outside. Until you are able to project it, you will continue to need external light to see. The world is only a projection of your being, or more precisely what you believe is your being. You are an entity of light and if you truly believed to be so, you could perceive this space as clearly as if you were a sun within these walls. But you do not, and thus you project that belief outside of yourself and regard this place as dark, void of other sources of light.

This was something so far from the common way of thinking that I'm sure my expression was beyond incredulous.

There are martial arts masters who can easily defeat adversaries when blindfolded. Some of them can even hit a perfect bull's eye with an arrow at a distance of many yards without using their sense of sight. How do you think these things are possible? No scientist in your world has found an explanation for these phenomena, and yet there are numerous examples. These are people who see, but without their eyes.

"They probably have some special gift or natural talent," I replied, my feeble hypothesis evaporating as soon as I uttered it.

Not at all. You could do it too. It would take years of arduous training—that's for certain—but no special gifts are needed. All human beings possess these skills but they have forgotten they have them.

He brought his face close to mine and lowered his voice, as if he were about to share a great secret.

The truth is you do not believe you have this ability and it is precisely your lack of trust that makes it impossible for you to access a different level of perception. You are dreaming of a reality that simply obeys your desire, and your desire is to not remember you possess this ability, at least for now. You are a god of such power that you can even choose to forget that you are. However you are here to remember and one day the memory of who you truly are will come to you. Most likely, other lives will be necessary, but you will eventually come to remember because this is the aim. It is the only one for which you have decided to dream and experience this reality.

My eyes were becoming used to the dimness and they met with the master's penetrating look. It only took me a second to realize I couldn't hold that gaze. Instinctively my eyes shifted elsewhere for a more comfortable place to rest. In front of me sat the proof of how much a man's eyes reflect the level of his interior being and my difficulty engaging with his revealed the immense abyss that existed between us. Or at least that's what I thought.

Noticing how I averted my eyes, he cocked his head slightly to one side.

Whatever hypothesis you make about why you have difficulty holding my gaze will be incorrect. There is no difference between your being and mine. Each one outwardly manifests exactly what it believes to be, and if you believe you occupy an inferior level on the scale of personal evolution compared to me, then this is what you will experience. Not because it is the absolute truth but because, as I have told you, you are creating a reality that mirrors your most intimate beliefs.

I began to ponder what I had just heard, expecting him to pause, but he continued with greater emphasis.

Just as all other things that surround you, I too represent a projection of your being. This means you see in me what belongs to you: my wisdom is your wisdom. The fact that you can recognize wisdom is clear proof that it is inside you, in some hidden and as yet unexplored corner—a much greater being than you can even remotely imagine is there.

His wisdom is my wisdom? I had never thought of it in those terms. I had read about the Law of Mirrors but had never taken it to this degree. In fact, whenever I'd heard someone explain it, they generally referred to it with regard to the negative characteristics we don't like in others. Instead, this way to conceptualize one of the laws of the universe was completely new to me, and the master must have sensed it.

You cannot appreciate the beauty of a panorama or a work of art if that beauty is not already present inside you. Equally, you cannot notice the wisdom of a person if that wisdom does not belong to you as well. The world you see is what you are creating by projecting outwardly the characteristics of your being. You must stop believing that things exist independently from you.

You are the cause of your dream, not the effect. A dream cannot exist without a dreamer and thus the wisdom you see in another cannot exist except as a projection of your same wisdom.

Once again he presented me with the idea that I was living inside a dream. Various theories I'd read on the illusory nature of reality flashed in my mind. For example, I knew that according to quantum physics, at a microscopic level, matter doesn't exist until an observer decides to observe it; before then each particle is only a wave of probability. However, the idea that it was all a dream conflicted directly with my understanding of reality as being what we experience through the five senses.

I'd never studied these concepts in depth—I'd always seen them as curiosities to delve into some day—but as I sat there I realized I couldn't put off facing them any longer. Right from the beginning, in fact, the master had presented me with a totally different vision of the world, one based on the idea that earthly experience is nothing more than an illusion created by the mind. I assumed it was a fundamental tenet of the Tibetan doctrine since he seemed to base most of his teaching on it.

I had indeed meditated on the question during my practice the day before and had a multitude of things to ask him. More than anything, I hoped he would shed light on some of what I saw as contradictions.

"Master," I began, "if everything I see around me is only fruit of a dream, who's dreaming? Am I supposed to assume that I don't exist and that I'm only a fantasy in the mind of someone else?"

He shook his head slowly.

You are asking the wrong question. This is your ego speaking and it is expressing all of its concern for its survival. When you say 'I', you are speaking of an entity that does not exist. That which you call 'I' is only the sum of all the experiences that are in your memory, and you hold onto them desperately to create an identity for yourself. But it is only a trick of your ego that makes you believe you exist as a being separate from the rest of the world. The world does not exist; only your world does. It is composed exclusively of your past and it exists only in your memory. It has nothing to do with who you truly are.

As a result, you have come to believe in an infinity of things that do not exist: the concept of I, my, your; past and future; right and wrong. You are prisoner of a dream in which you dream things that do not have any real substance. However we have already spoken about this. Today I want to speak about other aspects of the dream.

Confusion claimed me once again. Fortunately, when the master continued, his tone was reassuring, perhaps to underline the positive message he was about to give me.

You exist—of course you do—but not in the form you believe. Actually, your true being does not have form. You are neither something nor someone. You are, and that is all. You are neither your body nor your mind. They too are part of the dream since they are fruit of the illusion you are creating. You asked who is dreaming. Naturally, it is your true self but do not try to imagine what that is because one cannot understand it with intellect or reason.

"How can I not imagine it?" I protested, my voice a little too loud for a library. "The mind needs some sort of representation to understand a concept. For example, I imagine my true self as an immense being of light, inside or above me. I know that it's not the right image, but I have to..."

I abruptly stopped speaking. The master was looking at me with a surprised expression, as if caught off guard by my sudden reaction. His face softened and I could feel his willingness to try and understand my frustration, triggered by concepts lightyears from anything I had ever faced before. He looked at me serenely for several seconds. By that point, I had learned that it was so I would pause for reflection, allowing me time to find my necessary center again and be ready to continue listening to his words.

There is no right or wrong image. If you wish to visualize your self you are free to do so. What is important is to distinguish between the one who observes and the observed object. What you are striving to visualize is the one who creates the dream, and at the same time observe the dream itself in order to experience it. Therefore, your true self is he who observes.

In the moment when you try to visualize your true self, your mind is forced to compare it to something you know, for example a being of light in your case. That is what a mechanical mind does: in order to understand, it looks for an image of reference from its past. There is no reason to regret this because it is normal. Anything you can imagine on a rational level, in fact, must inevitably already be catalogued by your mind, otherwise you cannot visualize or conceive of it—something from your known world, in other words from your past.

I had never considered that the world known to me is made up of things that belong to my past. I'm unable to conceive of anything else and therefore use the images I've already memorized. Like Lego blocks, I can build anything I want but only within the limits of what is possible with the set of blocks I have in my hands.

The observer cannot be tied to the past: the past exists only in your dream and the observer lives outside of it, beyond time and space. To be able to grasp your own observer you must bring it back to your mind and give it form, thus making it one of the many manifestations of your dream. In that precise instant, however, you will lose it: the observer will cease to exist and will become the object under observation.

It is like trying to capture the moon reflected in a puddle. When you reach toward the image, the water—disturbed by your hand—ripples and breaks the reflected image, the gesture suddenly in vain. Thus, you discover that the reflection of the moon is not the moon.

This is why the observer cannot be observed and why it is not worth trying to imagine him. Just as I instructed you before, in order to discover who you truly are ask yourself the question, and then dismiss each idea as it comes to you.

"I tried to do that last evening, master. But instead of feeling better, I started thinking that I'll never come to know my true self."

It is not necessary to come anywhere. You have reached the destination: you are already your true self. You cannot know him because knowing implies that you are two distinct subjects: the one who knows and the one who is known. Instead, you and your true self are the same thing; you are indivisible. The eye cannot see itself, likewise perception cannot be perceived.

The only thing you can try to do is feel that you are your true self. You can only silence your mind and identify yourself with him, clearing the fog that keeps you from truth until you perceive there is no separation. You cannot observe your true self, you can only be it.

Again, he brought his face close to mine and looked deeply into my eyes.

If you want to experience your true self, instead of limiting yourself to silencing your mind when you practice meditation this evening, dedicate your attention to total contemplation of yourself.

I had the feeling an important revelation was coming, so I quickly glanced at my tape recorder to be sure it was on. I didn't want to miss a single word.

Observe your thoughts in a detached way, as if they do not belong to you. Let yourself go, without judging or holding back. There is no need to pose resistance. If you leave yourself out of your thoughts, you will see that slowly they become fewer and less frequent. Then observe the interval between one thought and another, fixing all your attention on that brief moment of silence. You will discover that your true nature is silence itself, which is made of pure awareness. You will become that silence and will become one with it. You must become aware of your awareness, and feel that it is your only true essence.

He continued to stare into my eyes, holding my full attention with such intensity that my rational self was anesthetized. I couldn't pull my eyes away from his gaze, as if he had opened a direct channel into my mind and through which he transferred all his immense knowledge.

Perceive that state of immutable and silent attention which is at the base of any thought that appears in your mind. That is your awareness, the door to access your true being. It exists before and regardless of any other thought or perception. It is the white screen on which the entire film of your existence is projected. Feel yourself at one with it and you will understand which direction to take to conduct your search. That awareness is you. The path to your awakening must pass through that door.

What I have just revealed is the true meaning of meditation. It is a priceless gift, make a treasure of it. Few people come to understand that the wise man does not meditate to search for himself, but to be himself.

He sat, unmoving, staring at me for several more interminable seconds, as if he wanted to be sure his words were well set in my mind. Then he rose slowly to his feet and gestured for me to do the same. I struggled to focus again on my body and surroundings as I slowly emerged from the semi-hypnotic state I was in. I stood up, resting my hand on the tabletop to steady myself, and followed him toward the center of the enormous, dark room, and from there through a corridor between two tall bookcases full of volumes. I could sense the weight of knowledge contained in the tomes and it infused the atmosphere with solemn sacredness.

Who knew what and how much wisdom the volumes held? I imagined that many of them had remained protected from the eyes of the world since time immemorial. I felt a slight sense of envy for the master and those like him who had the privilege of accessing such immense wealth. Would an entire lifetime even be enough to read just one-tenth of the books my eyes beheld? About midway along the row of shelves, he stopped and turned toward me. With a sweeping gesture, he indicated the books that surrounded us.

Thanks to the meticulous work of monks who have lived in this ancient monastery through the centuries, this place holds ancient knowledge handed down from generation to generation.

Some books are written in languages that have by now been forgotten and that no one can interpret, while others have faded over time until they have become illegible. However this does not diminish their immense value. Not even a bit. If someone wrote them, it was so that the knowledge they contained could be revealed to the world and, in the precise moment they were written, that knowledge became part of universal awareness. It will never be lost, even if the words that describe it are no longer legible.

At first I couldn't understand how this was possible, but then I remembered having read that in several instances the same invention or scientific discovery was conceived simultaneously in two distant places by people who had never come into contact with each other. Some people hypothesize the existence of a global consciousness that contains all human knowledge and to which we are all constantly connected, even if only on an unconscious level. Could this be what the master was referring to? I felt excited considering they might be one and the same.

I imagined getting my hands on only a few of those books. What a thrill it would be! Before I knew it, I heard my own voice: "Master, I would very much like to access even only a small part of ..."

I didn't finish my sentence because he furrowed his brow and lifted his hand to silence me. I could do nothing but listen.

Do not regret the books you have not read or will never read. Regret negates your immense power. Listen, for I wish to reveal an important truth. Silence your mind and stop trying to apply reason to my words.

I inhaled slowly, paused, then let the air flow from my lungs.

These books, even if you believe you have never read them, were written by you. The entire universe is within you. Never forget this. Every event that occurs in your life, every master you encounter, every book you open was willingly placed on your path by your true self, available to you as you travel toward the realization of your true essence.

You already know many of the books in this library. They have been part of your being for ages, even if they are written in languages neglected for centuries. Other books contain information that would not be helpful for you in this moment since you would be unable to absorb them on a rational level. Therefore, do not regret the books you will not read or the master you will not meet. You have designed everything impeccably and will read only the right books at the right time, with the single aim of increasing your awareness.

He paused, adjusted the drape of his robe over his left shoulder, and gazed at me as I tried to give meaning to his words.

As long as you deny this, you will deny your power since each of your thoughts and every one of your beliefs is an absolute and inviolable law for the universe. And you will risk making it impossible to access and manifest that power. Remember, the power is yours, and you also have the power to ignore it.

What did he mean I had written all those books? He had told me to avoid using rationale to explain what was evidently beyond all rational logic, and I tried. But I still couldn't understand. "Maybe if I could read something I could grasp what you're telling me. Then tomorrow, if it's alright with you, I could ask questions."

I knew you would ask for something to read. Your mind is confused and therefore it is searching for something to hold onto, to bring things back within your usual schemes. What I am telling you, in fact, is not part of your past experiences, at least not yet.

The road toward realization of the self must pass through the annulment of one's own past. Indeed, the purpose of telling you these things is to demolish in your mind everything that is part of your known world. Accept the confusion, do not resist it. Only through it can you construct a new awareness. A new building is not erected without first knocking down the old one that occupied the land. I understand your confusion, but this is the path to follow. Come with me and I will give you what you have asked for.

He turned and continued walking between the tall bookcases that were not much more than an arm's length apart. I followed silently, rejoicing in my heart for what he was about to concede to me. We stopped in front of a shelf that appeared untouched for centuries and he extracted a small book with a stiff brown cover and tied with a red ribbon. He blew delicately on it to eliminate some of the dust.

He held the book out to me as one does when offering a gift.

Do not open it until you are in your room. Its contents will probably surprise you, but try to remember our conversation here in the library. Perhaps then you will understand. Go now for your meditation practice and I will see you at the evening meal with the other disciples.

He bowed his head and pointed me in the direction of the great door. Our meeting for that morning was concluded. I returned his bow and walked as calmly as I could toward the exit, hugging the precious book to my chest with both hands.

THE RIGHT BOOK AT THE RIGHT TIME

When we consider a book, we mustn't ask ourselves what it says but what it means.

-Umberto Eco

I passed through the great room of the monastery, my breath quick and short in anticipation. I took the steps toward the dormitory two at a time, climbing as quickly as I dared. My sandals and long robe threatened to trip me up as I progressed, my hands occupied with clutching the book close to my heart. Once inside my room, I was surprised to find that there was a bowl on the table containing something warm and steamy and some fruit next to it, although it was early for lunch. The master must have made arrangements for my midday meal so I could read and carry out my daily meditation without needing to go out to eat. I wasn't hungry yet and the desire to read that book was so great that I decided to ignore the food. I could eat later.

If the master chose that book, he must believe its contents were truly important for me. Had other westerners been allowed access to the knowledge kept in the monastery's library? Maybe I was the first one to finally have the immense privilege. That certainly would be something to tell my grandchildren someday, I thought proudly. Excited like a child in front of a long-awaited gift, I pulled at the knot that held the ribbon and wondered what language the book might be written in. The cover held no title, so no hint there. He knew I couldn't read a text in an oriental language so hopefully it was in English or at least some other western language.

Finally I undid the knot and opened the book. The first pages were blank, as books bound by hand often are. I continued to turn the pages, looking for the first page of text but found nothing. Every page was blank, just like the one before. I quickly leafed through the pages again, thumbing the edge of the book. Front to back and back to front in hope of finding at least one page with something written on it. I held it closer to the tiny window, hoping the problem was a lack of illumination. Nothing. The master had given me a completely blank book. My heart felt like a stone as it sinks in a pond.

What was the message he was trying to tell me, assuming there was one? What were the words he'd used to tell me about the book when he gave it to me? I took out my tape recorder and rewound until I got to the moment when he placed the book in my hands. *"Its contents will probably surprise you, but try to remember our conversation here in the library. Perhaps then you will understand."* What did he mean by that? Could it have something to do with him saying I was the author of all the books in the library? But a book with nothing written in it doesn't need an author. I spent a long time trying to decipher the hidden meaning of the blank book but couldn't come to any conclusion that made sense.

Maybe that was precisely the problem. I tried again to understand its significance but this time took the stance of the observer. Eventually, with patient reflection, I came to the realization that I had been applying reason. I was holding onto my rational mind. Before coming to the monastery it was the only way I knew to resolve problems. But thanks to the master's teachings I was beginning to see that the mind can only formulate hypotheses based on what's contained in memory. Perhaps he wanted me to have this experience as a way to nudge me toward understanding that nothing new can emerge from simply remixing the past. Whatever experiences I'd had in the past were useless—I was facing a situation that was totally alien to my way of reasoning.

Since there was nothing to read in the book and I wanted to be a good student, I figured I could continue with my meditation exercises. The master had said to analyze my sensations and to observe my mind with detachment, being as conscious as possible of its internal mechanisms. So that's what I would do. I quickly ate the meal on the table then settled on the bed in a comfortable position. With my eyes closed, I began to observe my thoughts and let them flow in and out without any interference, just as he'd instructed.

Understandably, my mind went immediately back to the blank book. I formulated what the master had called hypotheses, trying to find some plausible significance. As I did so, I realized how my mind had been trying—in vain—to draw logical conclusions from the information at hand. This natural and completely adequate mechanism was probably fine for situations requiring a decision based on known facts, but how could it be the right tool when I had a problem in front of me that was so profoundly outside my life experiences? I sensed that I'd been letting my mind work as if on automatic pilot, always applying the same schemes of thought, even when the results I wanted seemed to elude me.

Even though I still had no idea what the real meaning of the book was, I felt I was beginning to learn how to observe in a detached way what happened inside me when faced with an unusual situation. Practice was finally beginning to yield results. It was exciting to discover that just by observing my mind in a detached way—not the mechanical, sleep-like interaction I normally had with my surroundings—the idea of being 'awake' took on new meaning. What I'd thought was wakefulness maybe really was a state of profound sleep, as the master kept telling me. If I could continue to calm the background noise of my life, by observing with a detached mind, maybe I could get in touch with, what the master called, my true self, and this was something I wanted.

With this revelation I felt stronger and satisfied by my progress, but I wanted to know still more. I had to wonder if that wasn't perhaps at least one of the reasons why the master had given me the blank book—to inspire me to pursue more introspective work.

The hours that separated me from dinner passed quickly. I'd heard it said that during meditation the passage of time is perceived differently compared to how it is normally. Being completely involved in an activity that demanded all my attention, time seemed to flow like a swift river and boredom became only an abstract concept. In fact, I'd read somewhere that meditation actually slows down the aging processes of the body, as if the passage of time is momentarily suspended. Who knows, maybe that's why Tibetan monks live to such advanced ages.

When it was time to go down for dinner I felt pleasantly anxious and impatient to meet the master again. I had a lot of questions to ask. I crossed the great prayer room, passed through a colorful archway and stepped inside the dining hall for the first time.

Bright fabric draping hid the high ceiling from view, painted banners hung on the walls, and everything about the space suggested a festive atmosphere. There was no hint of incense, only the delicious aroma of wholesome food prepared simply. There was a great coming and going of young monks with bowls in their hands, brimming with God's bounty—rice, legumes, all types of vegetables, steaming soups—and trays piled high with fresh and dried fruit. A veritable feast for the eyes and, I expected, for the palate. Four rows of low tables parallel to one another occupied the room, each only about eight inches above the floor. Purple cushions provided seating. No one had sat down yet so I remained standing in a corner to observe, trying not to be an obstacle.

Standing there, I had the opportunity to again notice everyone's joyful expression. I guess I still wasn't used to seeing so many smiling people. Why were they all so happy? It was, as far as I knew, an evening like any other, just a normal dinner, not any different from the ones they consumed every day. The same people, the same room, the same routine—nothing special.

The words resonated in my head: *nothing special.* I stood there for a moment—observing—and it occurred to me that it doesn't take anything special for a person to feel joyful, and those smiling monks were tangible proof. In that moment I also understood another thing: joy, true joy, the pure type that is born from your heart, is contagious.

I surprised myself. I had only been there two days and I was beginning to think in new ways. Maybe it was because of the master's illuminating teachings, or the serene atmosphere of the monastery, or the meditations I did every afternoon, or likely all these things together. But whatever the reason, something in me was changing. As if a part of me was withering, making space for a completely new person, someone who saw life with different eyes. What would I be like when I returned home after the week was up, I wondered. The constant message that everything was simply an illusion led me to consider that life is a beautiful game, and that it's my job to enjoy the ride and externalize the joy I have in a natural way. Perhaps I hadn't yet gotten to the point of feeling unconditional happiness, but the mental peace and new vision I'd acquired were already staggering. I was grateful.

Suddenly, everyone in the room stopped what they were doing. I didn't understand what was happening but then I saw the master enter, followed by a group of monks. They looked like the same ones from the breakfast in the great room the day before. He sat at the center of the first of the four tables so he wouldn't have his back to anyone. Slowly, in a very orderly way, all the monks began to sit down on the cushions, apparently without any predetermined order or rule. I was still standing in my corner, waiting to understand where I could sit. Again, I felt a bit embarrassed because I didn't know if I was free to choose a place or if I should wait until someone told me where to go. My mind jumped back to what the master had said to me at our first meeting: my mind was working frenetically to try and pull itself out of an uncomfortable situation that was purely imaginary, fruit of useless and senseless mental cogitations. I took a deep breath and tried to observe my thoughts with detachment.

I was pulled out of my contemplation by one of the monks at the head table who waved to attract my attention. The place in front of the master was free and he was encouraging me to sit there. What luck! As soon as I lowered myself onto the cushion with my legs crossed under the table, the master made a sign and everyone pressed their hands together in front of the their faces, closed their eyes, and slightly bowed their heads until their foreheads touched the tips of their fingers. I rushed to imitate their gesture, although I wasn't sure exactly what they were doing. For that reason, I kept my eyes open just a crack so I could watch and follow their lead.

It looked like a ritual of thanksgiving for the food we were about to consume as they prayed or maybe recited a mantra. However, since the room was silent I wasn't sure. Obviously I couldn't interrupt to ask but instead let my mind observe.

All the religions I know of have a ritual of thanks for food. Here in this isolated monastery, on the slopes of the tallest mountains in the world, people were giving thanks not that dissimilarly from how people in many Western religions do. It occurred to me that perhaps the act of giving thanks came before the creation of individual religions, that it is even more ancient and truly important. Gratitude, as the master had taught me, is an act of great power.

With the moment of prayer concluded, the meal began. Before I even put food on my plate I asked, "Master, when I opened the book you gave me, I discovered it contains only blank pages. Nothing's written in it. What does it mean?"

He held his bowl out to the monk on his right. A serving dish piled high with rice was nearby and he was clearing asking for some. Once he set his bowl of rice in front of himself, he lifted his eyes to meet mine.

Do not stop at outward appearances. The book I gave you contains more information than you can imagine. You must learn to look past the veil of your rational mind to glimpse the true meaning of things. Every object, word, or event is nothing more than a symbolic representation of some deeper concept, the meaning of which goes well beyond what the mind can see through the eyes. You believe you live in a world of things and people but in reality you are living in a universe that is made of symbols. That blank book is one of them.

"Please, master, tell me the book's hidden meaning. I thought about it all afternoon but didn't come up with a logical explanation," I blurted.

That book came into your hands to point out your habit of creating expectations. They are the result of your propensity to make assumptions. This morning you took for granted that your knowledge would be amplified by reading some of the books found in the library. I sensed your excitement about gaining access to that immense body of knowledge and how you assumed personal growth could derive from the accumulation of the wisdom contained there. Instead, you are unaware that you will begin to grow only when you question everything you think you already know.

You live in an illusory world in which you are the only artifice of the dream you are dreaming. Even though you know this truth, you are unable to bring yourself out of it. There are two categories of dormant beings. Those in the first group, which is made up of the greatest number of people, struggle to demonstrate with all their strength the truthfulness of their illusory world. They are people who are destined to fail because it is impossible to pass off as true something which is not. Those in the other group, like you, have sensed that perhaps they are living in an illusion of their own creation and they struggle in that dream to find proof and validation of their intuition. Also these people are destined to fail because they look for truth on the outside, as I have already told you, often in books or a guru. They will never get anywhere because those books and those gurus are also part of the dream.

Always remember that you are the origin of everything and therefore you are the one who decides what is your truth. This is the great secret, and when everything is finally clear you will laugh freely and full-heartedly about it, remembering when you struggled uselessly to find 'the truth'. That blank book puts in front of your eyes the fallaciousness of your world, with its false assumptions and useless expectations that duly will not be satisfied, just as you were disappointed in seeing that the book, which you expected great things from, contained nothing.

You must comprehend that the suffering, the malaise which often appears in your mind, derives only from your foolish assumptions and subsequent expectations. Abandon them and you will feel lighter, as if you let go of heavy ballast that weighs on your inner existence. That ballast is made of your past and it materializes through beliefs and expectations that can never find validation in real life. It renders you blind and keeps you from accessing the ultimate truth, the only one that can give you joy. All the answers are inside of you because you are truth. Never forget this.

So, he was saying I needed to eliminate expectations in order to eliminate suffering. Once again the master astonished me. I would never have been able to grasp this concept of life without the help of the wordless book he gave me. At that point, however, another question came to mind. "If I'm the origin of everything and all the answers are inside of me, why then do I feel a strong need to read books and follow the teachings of masters?"

The problem is that you have stopped asking yourself questions, and that is because you assume many things. Assuming you already have the answers leads you to erroneously believe there is no need to pose questions to yourself. You think they are superfluous. Ever since you were a child you learned to suppress the voice of truth that came from your being. On the rare moments when you did ask yourself a question you were deaf to the answer. Your mind is perennially busy reasoning with logic to draw conclusions, starting from the false presuppositions you think are real. That reasoning however cannot provide you with a reply because the answer is burrowed deep in your past from which nothing new can emerge. That mechanism constantly tugs at your attention and directs it outwards, and this drives you further from the ultimate truth.

The only true answer can come from your true self, but you must silence your mind and listen to your sensations if you want to hear it. *Your mind and your sensations will be the ones to tell you if what you are reading or listening to is truly what you are looking for. You already know the truth, but you have to listen to the quiet signals that come from your being to be able to recognize it.*

Remember what I told you in the library this morning: you are the author of all those books. Reading books and listening to masters is not how you learn, it is how you remember the things you have always known. Only what is true will vibrate deeply in your being. Therefore, learn to recognize these signs.

His words were clear enough but I wanted him to understand why I had asked to read something from the library. I hoped to provide him with a plausible justification for my insistent request. "I asked to read a book, master, because you yourself told me that the monastery's library holds knowledge that has been handed down through the centuries and preserved thanks to the meticulous collection work of the monks."

He grinned, evidently amused.

Calm your mind and realize that you are only looking for rational motivation behind a need of the soul. The reason for your request is clear to me. You are the one who is not able to attribute true meaning to it. A thirst to rediscover your true nature is what led you to undertake this trip. That unstoppable impulse to always want to know more comes from the impetus exercised by your true self, which has as its single goal that of returning to its origins to understand itself. There is nothing that needs justification and it makes no sense to offer resistance. You must only be cheered by it and indulge your desire, savoring the beauty of this fantastic voyage and the infinite joy you get from it.

Abandon every impulse to decide what will be your next book or who will be your next master. They will manifest themselves spontaneously, and each time you will receive, in that precise instant, what you need to foster your growth. This rule is valid for any event in your life. Joy derives only from renouncing the desire to control what happens at all costs.

"Master," I replied, "I get that it makes no sense to try and control the events in my life, but then I feel impotent in the face of what goes on around me. If, as you say, I'm a divine being, I would imagine I can somehow influence things and choose to experience what I desire most. You said that free will translates into the freedom to choose where to place one's attention in order to experience it. I don't understand how this goes with renouncing the desire to control things?"

It depends on what type of control you intend to apply. You can exercise free will—it is your divine right—but that does not mean control, only the exercising of a choice. Listen carefully. Your task is to declare your choice and then make sure you are ready.

He paused and stared into my eyes, but I wasn't grasping the full meaning of his words. I didn't get what he meant by being ready.

I believe you are beginning to understand that the right book comes at the right time.

I nodded.

It comes into your hands because you are ready for what it contains and it is the same for a choice. When you are ready to accept that choice, the desire will become manifest. This is true for all the events of your life whether they bring you joy or great sorrow. In the moment that you make a choice, only the experience you are ready to receive will occur.

I couldn't comprehend his leap from a book to a choice.

There are two levels of reality: a material one that corresponds to what you experience with your five senses, and another one that is immaterial and made up of vibrations and corresponding forms of thought which are the true and only cause for what is manifest at the first level. You can manifest in the first level only what is aligned to your current vibration in the second level. This is what I mean when I say you need to be ready. Alignment can occur involuntarily, such as when a point of attraction is determined by your current level of growth, or voluntarily, like in the case of an event you desire to have manifest. You can choose what experience to be ready to receive, simply by aligning yourself with the corresponding form of thought.

To be ready means choosing to be what you desire to experience. Become one with the world you wish to experience. There is no other course.

"Alright, but excuse me, master," I objected, "the way I see it, choosing what you wish to experience means, essentially, trying to exert some sort of control."

Before replying he shook his head slightly.

Choosing to be is very different from exerting control. I can tell this difference is not clear for you and this explains why you are unable to comprehend what I am revealing. First exists the desire, which you simply express by 'choosing' to be what you want to experience and accepting at the same time the result of a previous choice, what is already manifest. Instead, you attempt to exert control when you refuse what is manifest in the here and now and try to modify through action what does not satisfy you. This type of control is impossible to attain and any attempt to operate in such way will be inexorably destined to fail.

Look at the table before you. It is lavish with a great variety of dishes and you are free to choose anything you wish to eat. The awareness of being able to choose what you desire does not elicit a need to complain about the presence of some dishes which you do not like. Thus it shall be with the events of your life when you finally comprehend your enormous power to choose.

You will not be able to exercise that power however without first understanding that choice and control do not act at the same level. You exercise your choice when you function at the second level, that is at the immaterial level. Instead, you try to exercise control when you act at the first level, with the illusion of being able to modify what is already manifest in some way. This is the only understanding you need regarding the mechanisms that create reality, nothing more.

If I understood, the master was saying that choosing is not the same as controlling because choosing means accepting everything that is manifest. I'd never thought of choosing and accepting as being related—it was an extraordinary concept. I was excited because I was finally getting insight on how people create their own reality, and another clear and reasonable explanation of what I had already read about the Law of Attraction.

Dinner concluded and the master stood up. The monks who had accompanied him at the beginning of the meal prepared to leave the table, and I stood up as well.

THE REAWAKENING

Awake. Be the witness of your thoughts. You are what observes, not what you observe.

Buddha

Everyone moved into the great prayer room where steaming teapots waited on the various carpets with each pot surrounded by about a dozen cushions. I was strongly motivated to continue our discussion so I followed the master, hoping to be able to sit next to him. I had travelled thousands of miles to be there, to listen to his precious teachings, and I didn't want to let the opportunity slip away. I quickly realized that, once again, my mind had set to worrying for no reason and tried to calm it. The master settled himself on one of the cushions and he gestured to the cushion closest to him. Of course, I didn't hesitate.

Almost immediately, a young disciple stepped forward, picked up the teapot and, beginning with the master, poured tea into the cup in front of each person. His movements were pleasing and had a ritual-like air. Each time he prepared to pour the tea, he made a small bow to the recipient, poured, then bowed again. He smiled broadly and directed his expression of joy toward the person before him. It was a pleasure to watch but I felt a little uncomfortable being served and treated so graciously so I asked the master to explain more about what I was witnessing.

Distance from your mind hasty conclusions. The disciples of this monastery are learning that there is no separation between one's being and the surrounding world. These gestures of courtesy are performed with absolute joy, with the conviction that any act of love toward another is in reality an act of love toward the self. By savoring, moment by moment, a sense of belonging to an enormous divine plan, they are filled with bliss and that is what you see in their eyes. They have no doubt about being integral and irreplaceable parts of that plan. Through these gestures of pure love for others, the disciple learns to love himself, recognizes his own divine nature, and sees it reflected in others. The reverence they demonstrate is nothing more than a recognition of the divine essence that permeates the entire Creation.

I was about to thank him for his thorough explanation but didn't get the chance because he continued speaking.

Your soul has perceived the spontaneity of the disciple's gift and has rejoiced in it as an authentic act of love. Indeed, for a moment it brought you well-being, but then your mind stepped in and brought to the surface a sense of guilt buried in your unconscious. You have become accustomed to not receiving and this makes you feel uncomfortable every time someone shows you a gesture of courtesy.

If you want abundance to enter into your life, you must learn to receive and experience all the joy that derives from it. However, to be able to do so you must eliminate that long-standing sense of guilt. You will succeed in doing so only when you are able to love yourself unconditionally. This is what the disciples learn through this practice. Your eyes see a disciple serving tea; a wise man sees an exchange of infinite love in which the giver receives much more than he imparts. The disciple knows this law and also knows that love cannot be found in books. Unconditional love must be practiced.

With the last sentence, he lifted his index finger and looked at me with great seriousness, as if urging me to consider the practice of unconditional love fundamental. This wasn't the first time he'd emphasized the need to practice what one wants to learn. I remembered that he'd also taught that reading books is important but remains an end unto itself if it's not experienced through practice.

I realized that every episode in the monastery, even the most trivial, offered me precious opportunities to receive teaching. My initial sense of being ill at ease in that unknown environment and desire to go back home were only distant memories by that point, almost as if they didn't belong to me any longer.

What I really wanted in that moment was to continue the discussion the master had begun regarding abundance and how to allow it to enter one's life. "Master, if I understand correctly, in order to attract what I desire I have to first resolve my sense of guilt," I began, "and that it's important to learn to receive without those guilty feelings. You said it's important to be ready by aligning myself with my desires. So, if I do these things will I attract abundance? Is this all it takes?"

The corners of the master's lips lifted to hint at a smile.

"I knew that sooner or later you would ask the question again—Westerners yearn to accumulate earthly goods. Perhaps you have read books that declare that the way to reach happiness is through the possession of material things. In a certain sense, this has not been a mistake. Many people have been attracted toward a path of growth by playing on this longing to reach happiness through possession.

In the Grand Plan, all means are considered—even those that may be seen as less pure or less spiritual—in order to initiate the greatest number of people in this path toward reawakening. Those who are ready, however, come to realize along the way that the true objective is something else. At that point they begin to move toward the only true objective:

rediscovery of their own divine nature. You cannot expect someone to renounce their earthly desires until they are ready because attachment is one of the fundamental steps along the path. Woe to he who pretends to be illuminated but suppresses his desires with force. One can begin to climb a ladder only starting from the very first rung.

Therefore, I understand your question and shall reveal to you something very important..."

He paused to sip his tea and I waited for him to continue, agape like a child listening to a fantastic fable.

He set his cup down slowly.

All those who believe they can attract events or things to themselves or create their own reality make a great mistake. They lose sight of the true nature of the world. I have already explained that the entire universe is within you, and you have insisted on portraying it in spatial terms, imaging yourself enormous like the universe. Well, my statement also applies to time because it too is generated in your mind and therefore it is part of the same illusion. You are an immense being that encompasses all the universe—past, present and future. This means that any event you can imagine already exists within you, and therefore it makes no sense to think of 'attracting' or 'creating'.

If you feel you need to attract reality to you, you are affirming your separateness from it, and this affirmation corresponds to a command to the universe. The problem is that you cannot have control over that which you believe is separate from you.

If this was the case, the books I'd read up until then had told me a false truth. "Master, this revelation is astonishing, but what exactly do I have to do to materialize my desires?"

It is very simple. Enter into the idea of being the entire reality. Everything already belongs to you; there is nothing to create. This is the great secret that no book in your world has ever revealed to you. Many books will say that visualization is the tool to attract the events you desire, but there is nothing further from the truth. Visualization is useful, but the purpose of it is completely different from what you have always believed.

Do not assign other purposes to visualization other than being happy in the here and now. Any other use of visualization is only superstition. Perhaps you are now beginning to understand what aligning yourself with your own desires means. Being well and feeling joy in the here and now anchors your desires in the present moment and helps you recognize that you are at one with them and with the whole universe. Desires are already yours in the present instant, you need not do anything else but rejoice in them.

Use visualization to be well in the here and now? As if it could be a refreshing massage for the mind... The simplicity of this concept was as disconcerting as it was disarming. Perhaps what the master was saying was that positive emotions come from visualization and from there comes the opportunity to align your desires. And maybe that's why the urge to obtain things does nothing but generate the opposite effect. Thinking that we need to attract to ourselves what we desire is, I guess, a way then of declaring a separation from it and that, in turn, just denies the power to obtain it. If only there were an instruction manual for how to use our immense power to its fullest!

I was so excited by what I was beginning to understand that words jumped out of my mouth before I was aware of thinking them. "This experience at the monastery is more than I could have ever envisioned and I feel so fortunate to receive your teachings. Can I come back in the future to meet you again?"

It does not depend on me—I exist only in your mind. You could choose to not meet me anymore, dream of meeting another master, or perhaps seek out one who is wiser than me. Your question derives from the premise that I am real, and that this monastery and everything you see have true substance, independent of you. However, now you know that it is not so. You are in a dream and you may remember who you are through the teaching of any master you choose. When you wake up, you will remember my teachings but you will realize that this dream is only a trick played on you by your true self to bring what you already knew to your superficial mind. You are in this dream to remember truth and I will disappear when my task is complete.

Okay, it was all a dream, if that was what he wanted to call it. But what did he mean when he said he'd disappear? "Master, do you mean that if I return here next year, I won't find you? Or that this monastery won't be here?" I shook my head, not wanting to even think of the possibility.

I am here only because you are imagining me. I am your projection. I have no past and I will not have reason to exist when you no longer need me. You believe you are dealing with people who exist outside of yourself and who have their own stories. This is how you think about all the people who enter your life, but it is not so. You are in a dream and everything that is part of it materializes as needed. If it is difficult for you to believe this, think of a dream you have while sleeping. Have you ever believed that perhaps the people in that dream really had a past, and that they continued to exist in the morning after you awoke? You would, without doubt, reply negatively to this question. Yet, this is also what happens in the life that you call 'real'.

You are the origin of everything, never forget it. In the precise instant when you say 'I am', an entire universe comes to light to reflect this statement of yours and make it possible for everything you believe in to materialize with the single purpose of experiencing it. This is the true origin of the world you see, and its only aim.

Well then, if this is a dream, the same rules must apply as in the dreams I have at night, which however generally seemed much shorter. Yet there was something in the analogy that didn't make sense and so I asked, "How can this only be a dream created by myself, master, if I was born from two parents who existed before I came into the world?"

You are still assuming things which, upon careful analysis, could be revealed to be without basis. Do you remember the exact moment you came into the world? Would you be able to describe your first moments of life?

"Of course not," I replied, "but only because I was too young to remember."

The master hinted at a smile, a sign I'd come to understand meant I wasn't getting his point.

You have fallen so deeply into your dream that you can't see the reality of things. You are simply dreaming to be a person born in this time period, brought into the world by your current parents. Your dream began when you erroneously considered yourself a separate being. That is when a cycle of reincarnations began. Reincarnation is nothing more than focalizing, on the part of the observer, on a fictitious reality that, before the person enters it, he has imagined. Therefore every part of it, including parents, has been created by him or her. It is not possible to have knowledge of the moment in which the dream began, and that is why you cannot remember your first moments of life.

"Does this mean my parents don't exist? Are you saying they're only in my imagination?"

He smiled and, again, slowly shook his head.

This doubt persists because you still consider yourself a separate entity from your parents and from the rest of the world. We are all one single thing, belonging to a single consciousness, and each of our parents is a part of it too, differentiated to play a precise role in this reincarnation of yours. You will comprehend what I am telling you only when you accept the idea of not being separate from all you see.

Remember, the observer and the observed object are the same thing because they are indivisible. So long as you are in the dream and observe it, all your creations—including your body and the people you see around you—appear to exist. *When you awaken and stop observing the dream, everything that was part of it will disappear and what remains is the knowledge acquired through the experiences of the dream. Knowledge is the only real thing in that dream, and as such it has its own existence which goes beyond the dream itself. 'Learning' with the superficial mind serves nothing—everything else disappears together with the dream—and only knowledge acquired through experience will remain impressed in your being forever.*

"But my parents have memories of the time before my birth," I objected. "And they lived for many years before I came into the world. In fact, my father often told me about when he was a boy and he helped my grandfather, who was a farmer, to cultivate the fields."

You continue to confuse the dream of a hypothetical past time with experienced reality. You are dreaming of having a father who told you about his experiences when he was a boy. In other words, you have just told me an episode from your dream, but since you are not awake you are convinced that it really happened. Do not give actual significance to the past—not yours or that of others—because it cannot have it. Each memory exists only in the mind of the person who dreams of having remembered it. Could you indicate where one of your past days is located, if not in your mind? As the past and future are illusions, they are not real.

Only the present moment exists—the here and now—and contains within it all the past and all the future. In other words, the present is the cause of past and future.

"The present moment is the cause of the past? I don't get it. Master, you know I'm trying to understand but it feels as if it's just beyond my grasp."

You are the present, and since you are the origin of everything you are also the origin of the past. Every memory of yours, as well as everything that is part of what you believe is your past, exists only to validate what you are in the here and now. This is the only moment that exists. Your infancy, your first day at school, your first kiss, and all the other memories impressed on your mind are part of a single event that is taking place now, in this instant in this place. Those memories are ripples on the global consciousness and like tiny waves created by a stone dropped into a lake they propagate in all directions and exist simultaneously in the present moment. Just as the wavelets depend on the stone that was dropped, so do your past and future depend on your present—what you are in this moment. Change your being and your past and future will inevitably change.

I couldn't avoid asking the question that, I'm sure, anyone faced with the idea that his life was only a dream would ask. "Well then, if all this is an illusion created by our minds, what sense does it have to live? It could make somebody think that life has no sense, and that therefore it's without importance." The master pulled his bushy eyebrows down over his eyes, his expression stern.

I have spoken to you more than once about the importance of living this terrestrial experience. The aim is to return to our divine nature with a greater level of awareness than when we undertook this journey. We are here to discover what it means to be divine beings, but to do that we must pass through an experience which is not divine. This is why once we drop down onto this material plane we do not remember who we truly are. We are all part of the same consciousness that, through our innumerable experiences, is maturing the awareness of the true being.

Each life experience, even the smallest and least significant, is unique and diverse from all the rest. Your life is precious, without it there would be an unbridgeable gap of knowledge. You are an irreplaceable piece of an enormous puzzle. You must love life and protect it, in any expression in which it appears because it is the sacred manifestation of a divine plan. He who knows the true meaning of this existence—even if it is illusory—can only appreciate it and love it unconditionally. It is a lack of awareness that impedes people from loving and appreciating life, not the other way around. If you look carefully, you can see with your eyes the harmful effects of the deep unawareness in which humanity is immersed.

"Thank you for your comforting words, master, they encourage me to continue along this path. I have one more question. What can you tell me about death? When a person's body dies, does the illusion end and do they move on to some higher level of awareness?"

When you speak of death, I assume you are referring to death of the body, although understood in that sense it is only a relative concept which has a totally different meaning. Do not believe that death offers illumination, and not even that it is the end of everything. Your body can die but if your being is not reawakened, it will endure in the illusion of the dream and continue to create an illusory world, thinking it has an autonomous existence separate from everything else. In fact, many people die in their body but remain unaware of it, and they continue to create their world, thinking that they are still in material reality. True death is the death of the dual mind, that which creates your ego and your personality which makes you believe in separation.

Death of the mind is not a true death because it is the reawakening of the being. It represents the definitive end of the illusion and it can occur independently from the life of the body. It is the body's singular aim to facilitate death of the mind, and therefore fulfillment of the being. Therefore, honor your body because it is the fundamental and essential instrument to obtain reawakening. In the moment when the dual mind dies, time and space no longer have a reason to be. Remember, different from reality, illusion needs you to believe in order for it to exist. So, in the moment of true reawakening, the dual mind collapses and together with it the entire material universe disappears into nothingness because it is made of nothing. It is like darkness that disappears when illuminated. It is senseless to wonder where it has gone because it has never existed. As you see, therefore, your concept of death does not exist at all. Live your existence with joy in the certainty that your true self is an eternal being, and as such it has never been born nor will it ever die.

He gestured with his hand to one of the disciples who came to his side to help him stand up.

Now, go and rest. You have received much teaching today and you have many things upon which to meditate. Remember, your task it to spread this knowledge so that all of humanity may evolve. Treasure these teachings and do all that you can to carry out this mission.

He steadied himself then walked slowly toward the stairs without turning back, leaning on his disciple's arm for support.

I was truly astounded by all the incredible things he had revealed. He told me to carry my task to completion, but what exactly did he mean be that? Sadly, I had the sensation he was saying goodbye for the last time, as if we would never see each other again. With this thought in my mind, I climbed the stairs to my room and went to bed, the master's words whirling in my head as I fell asleep...

***

The sound of the alarm made me jump, yanking me into consciousness from a deep sleep. I turned off the irritating noise and sat on the bed. What was I doing at home in my bedroom? Where did my room in the monastery go? I looked at the clock: 6.30 a.m.

My airline ticket for New York was sitting on the bedside table and my suitcase was packed and waiting at the foot of my bed. The trip to Tibet, the monastery, the master... it was nothing more than a magnificent dream. I hadn't missed my flight, and my trip to New York was still there waiting for me – but it had all seemed so real! In fact, as real as the room I woke up in. How was it possible for my mind to come up with such a thing? Sitting there in my bed, words and details from the dream came back to me. For example when the master warned me that it's impossible to realize you're in a dream until you wake up and look at it from another level of awareness. I had to admit, it seemed he was right! What really struck me, though, was that if it had been a dream then the master's teachings must be fruit of my mind. *My wisdom is your wisdom...* I felt a quiver of recognition. Now it made sense. Knowledge is within us, we are already illuminated beings. Sometimes the true self devises tricks to put us in contact with that forgotten wisdom by materializing it in a book, or in a master as in my case.

I forced myself to stop thinking about the dream, I'd do that later. I had to get ready to go to the airport. I stood up, still a bit dazed, and took care of last-minute preparations. As I was about to put the voice recorder into my suitcase I noticed the memory was nearly full. Strange. I was sure I'd zeroed it the night before. I slipped it into my bag and made a mental note to check it during the flight.

I finished getting ready, picked up my things and left the house. Turning the key in the lock, I imagined the old man from my dream with a benevolent expression, watching me from above.

Remember? I told you it was all a dream...

APPENDIX: AUTHOR'S INSIGHTS

Hello, my name is Paolo Marrone and I would like to thank you for reading my book. This is a particular book, and I'm sure that many of you felt like there is something more behind the pages of this story. That's why I've decided to write this appendix, where we will go deep into the different meanings of the book and beyond what the Master explicitly revealed.

The book, at first sight, may appear to be complex, especially because of the different *'incredible revelations'*, if that's what we want to call them, which have been in contrast with the common belief of us citizen of the west.

Well, I have a confession: it seems like I haven't written this book...

It took two long years to complete it and during that time I suffered times of crisis because I had trouble *'reconnecting'* with my internal source of inspiration. I'm talking about connection because I believe there's no word that could explain better what happened every time I sat at my computer and typed. It may sound odd, but in different occasions, by re-reading the Master's sentences, I could not be more surprised of what I was capable of creating thanks to all that typing and I hardly recognize the paternity of what I was writing.

In my opinion, this book is the result of an inspiration coming from my connection to the "Global Conscience", a universal tank of knowledge to which every one of us and every moment can tap to, to take precious information that otherwise, with the only help of rational mind, we would never succeed to understand.

In this appendix I won't focus on my Master's teachings only, since I don't think they need a further explanation, also because everyone could extrapolate different lessons from those words. Like in any other lesson, indeed, the *grade of comprehension* varies depending on the *level of awareness reached* during each individual's growth.

I would like to share with you some of the aspects of this story with a specific meaning that may escape your attention at a first reading of the book.

Maybe some of you noticed, while reading the book, that the story that is told is nothing but the symbolic representation of a path leading to a personal growth. I would say that it can be considered a real *'initiatory path'*, symbolized by some peculiarities that follow.

As it is into the story, every one of us is called into a path of personal growth and very often thanks to events that may not be noticed by those who do not go into the details. A book, a video on the Internet or a meeting with somebody, all of those are possible excuses that our true self makes up to lead us towards our true nature. This is when that alarm doesn't sound, or the casual accident that happened to the wife of the man at the airport, they all represent casual events that can occur to those who are "ready" to be called.

Also, during that path of growth you are faced with moments when you are alone, sometimes overwhelmed by a feeling of despair. In fact in the book I'm find alone with myself thinking about what is happening in two different moments: at the bar, after the meeting with the old man, and later the first night at the monastery, where I'm left alone in my cell, with my mind filled with nostalgia, thinking about how far the world I knew and left was.

To enter a path of growth means to go on a journey toward far places, way further than our typical world, described by the usual aspects of our lives. The trip to Tibet is that jump into the void and a language which is hard to understand (you may recall it when I couldn't talk to anyone because I didn't know the language until my arrive at the monastery).

Another strong symbol is that time when I had to leave behind my watches and cellphones and that request when they wanted me to wear the typical disciple habit of that monastery once I had waken up. To start a path of growth, in fact, means to leave behind mental habits (represented in the book by technological objects), to walk in the shoes of a new person (the obligation to wear the maroon robe).

Some other symbols represent real aspects of our way of being. The first is that wonderful garden where the Master makes his first revelations. That garden represents an oasis of peace that is inside every one of us, and it can be accessed the first time only if you're showed by a wise hand, only to notice later that you've always had access to that place but that you could have never spotted the entrance door.

The big library is another important symbol. In the book I see that as a place full of knowledge very difficult to get access to (the dark at the entrance). That library represents the vast knowledge hiding behind every one of us, that none of us know it exists. That knowledge is something we already have (the Master says that I wrote those books), but we lost traces (the Master says that much of those books are written in dead or forgotten languages).

Also, do you remember me noticing that joy and serenity that described every person living in that monastery? Well, that happiness was already inside me, but I didn't know that I had it. The happiness that I didn't recognize manifested on the outside, projected onto those characters that I used to meet in that monastery. The message is everything we notice about others that also belongs to us, and our true self project that on the outside to have it in front of our eyes, so that we can recognize it.

Another important symbol that I want to analyze is represented by that white book that the Master gives me at the end of the visit at the monastery's library. Through that book the Master makes me understand that our path to personal growth is not made of storing new knowledge, but instead it is made of deleting false myths we've always believed in. Like it or not, those beliefs keep us constantly locked in a cage in our mind. But what is this cage like? How do we build it? How can we escape it?

What if I told you there are lots of cages, an infinite number, one inside another?

"You are entangled in a vicious cycle. You believe that you are separate from all that is, and as a consequence you

constantly create from nothing a dual world in the image of your erred belief, which is apparently separate from you. At the same time you observe your creation, forgetting that you are its creator, and fall into the illusion that what you see is reality. Your observation reinforces your beliefs, leading you to the illusion that you are right in believing that what you experience truly exists. And so on, further and further in an unending cycle. You have fallen so deeply into the spiral of your illusion that you can no longer perceive even the distant reflection of the place of light from which you came."

These are the words that the Master used in that monastery, explaining how did I fall in the spirals of a endless circle, so low that I can't perceive that place made of light where I come from.

Why did I choose these words? If we read closely, in that sentence the Master tells us effectively our condition of "sleeping" beings, deep in a spiral of apparently endless illusions. Those spirals are in fact walls in our mind we are surrounded of, real borders defining our world.

But what do we mean by "border defining our world"?

Let's begin by a simple concept: so that something can be perceived, it needs to be separated or able to be separated from everything. In other words, anything needs to have precise borders to exist, while on the other side there is everything that *'is not'* what we are looking at. We can't perceive a white object in a white world, unless we mark its borders with different colors all around it.

This is valid for an object, for our body, and of course for the entire world we live in. When I talk about world I mean everything that can exist for us and therefore what we can perceive, and we can be experienced about.

But the Universe has not boundaries, you would say. Potentially, it has but in reality things are a little different than what we image (or different from what we are told). Let's start by a presupposition that, based on quantic physics, only what we can have experiences about can exist, simply because without an Observator there is no observation. It has been established than that in every instant only there is what our Conscience can perceive.

That is our world, deep into an infinite potential quantum, where everything is possible, but in which only what we are able to perceive and conceive, happens. Therefore, there is no wall because those are made of what we find to be possible. In other words, that is what we believe to be the Truth.

There, we almost proved our point: those walls are made only by our conception of what is possible and impossible in our world. Those walls are made of beliefs or better, by the truths we believe in.

If we have the courage to go deep into this argument, we can finally understand what the Master meant by *"and so on, further and further in an unending cycle"*.

Why unending? After all, you'll say, if I make a work of growth that is intense and long, in the end I will be able to tear down those walls and make it out of the cage.

That's where the problem lies. There is no escape, or at least not in the direction we are looking at. Follow me: if that mental cage is made of our beliefs, our truths we believe are true, then there is no way out through acquiring new knowledge. Any other truth we believe in, won't be anything but an ulterior wall we will build to confine the world. Those are the spirals the Master talks about, and those are the concentric cages I'm talking about.

The breaking of mental cages can't happen by getting new truths. Those won't do anything but building new walls around us, confining us in a new world in which to believe.

I'll try explaining this another way:

The moment we accept new beliefs as true, since we are d we make them real in our lives. At that point we look at them saying "You see? That's the truth!", ignoring that we are experiencing that only because we made those and believe are real...

"And so on, further and further in an unending cycle" to use the Master's words.

How do we get out? The road is not *the one out*, towards getting knowledge, because after every wall we tear down we will find other walls we will build because of our new beliefs.

So, what do we do?

What if I told you that the only way is questioning everything you believe you know? Do you have the courage to do it? Because it takes courage, but it's the only way to break down the walls that keep us prisoners. We have to dismantle false beliefs that keep our nature in the dark in order to discover what we really are. This is the most truthful and important message of the Master.

So the only way out is *the one inside*, following the road that will lead us to find the truth in the only place where it can be, inside of us. Actually, as the Master said, the only way out is to understand we are the Truth. There is no truth to reach out there, if not the awareness of being immense, the one and the only created in the entire world we perceive, including the walls.

We are convinced that we have to learn something new in order to be able to begin our path of growth. It's not like that, as the Master wanted to prove by giving me that book with white pages.

So why do we read and stay informed?

Those who begin a path of personal growth, for sure they will feel a strong need of getting up to date, to read, to study, to know more and more. The feeling is like the Truth, capital T, written somewhere outside of us, and our job is to absorb as many information as possible, in order to fill that empty space of knowledge.

The Master in this book explains in different ways how this is not true, not in terms of approaching education about these subjects.

The main message to keep in mind is that, unlike what we made us believe from when we are born, we are deities, we came here to discover this great Truth through an earthly experience, via an apparent state of *non-deity*. This means that our True Self, what we really are, already knows everything. In a nutshell, we are enlightened beings already since this is our most intimate nature and essence.

The problem is that we don't know we are. Precisely, *we don't remember* we are.

I would like to focus for a brief moment on the etymology of the word *remembering*.

To remember comes from latin, *re-* (again, in the past) and *cor, cordis* (heart), so to bring something back to the heart.

Why is it so important to know the etymology of this word, what does the heart have to do with this?

Basically the approach we have to use when we are faced with any information about these subjects is that we don't have to take anything for true. In fact, we have to be close to our sensations, to what our heart feels it's true.

As I just said, we already know everything, hence we have to trust what our heart feels it's true when we read or listen to something. Even if it may seem odd, this is the right way towards discovering the enlightenment. Our self vibes in harmony with what it feels to be true, so we need to be guided by our sensations.

For example, the first time I read a book about the laws of attractions I was so excited by what I was discovering that I literally drop tears from my eyes. I had the feeling of knowing those things forever and I was stunned for not having considered what appeared to be so *obvious and granted* for me.

Somebody at this point may ask what is the reason why it is so important to read books or participate in seminars, since inside of all us we already know everything. It is important because we need somebody or something that helps us 'remember', indeed.

In my previous example it was obvious, as I learned later, that I've always known those information, but without that book it would have been difficult, if not impossible, to take them back to the surface of my awareness.

Trust no 'guru' who wants to make you believe you are incomplete and that you lack something to reach perfection. You already are a perfect being, since you are a deity, therefore everything that you need is somebody to help you 'remember it'.

All the truth is buried in our inside, under a multitude of preconceptions and beliefs that we have absorbed since our birth, thanks to what they taught us at school, in our family and in Church, etc.

You don't have to learn anything because of your True Essence and with it all your knowledge about Reality, is buried under a bunch of false bias, taboos, vetoes and inhibitions that makes you see a reality that actually doesn't exist.

The bad news is that those false truths affect every day of our lives, locking us inside a prison made of imaginary bars.

The good news is that the keys to that prison are in our hands.

So instead of learning new things, we have to demolish this big pile of false credence that stop our true essence from emerging. Let's put aside rationality, because it is based on that pile of false knowledge and cannot be helpful.

Let's use our heart instead, our sensations, to know whether something sounds to be true in our inside.

Let's face our personal growth and spiritual growth with our open mind and with the maximum curiosity, without prejudices or preconceptions, as a child would do.

This is what Jesus meant when he said:

"Let the little children come to me, and do not hinder them, for the kingdom of heaven belongs to such as these"

(Matthew-19,14)

Let's get our tools and start dismantling all of our current certainties. Let's doubt anything in order to let our True Self reach the surface who has been screaming for thousands of past lives, praying that someone could finally listen to it and make us Conscious again.

I would like to complete this appendix to this book with another important concept the Master stressed many times. It's about us being the only responsible for everything that happens. We are inside an illusion, nothing but a dream with open eyes. So who can be responsible for everything that happens in a dream if not the dreamers themselves?

Everything that is, is there because you created it, dear reader, including anything that comes across your path of personal growth, including this book, obviously. The Master, in that library, pointing at those books we were surrounded by, told me that I wrote those. Well, even if it may seem absurd, the Master with that sentence wanted to tell me that we are the only one responsible of what we experiment in our reality, and everything, just everything, has been put there to make our path of growth easier.

I don't know about you, but I always come across books, articles or seminaries that are perfect for that moment. I noticed that it's like there is a hidden director that determines every moment for every text, based on my level of personal growth and they organize events so that I could reach to them, one way or another.

Actually this happens for every event in our lives, because everything happens at the right time, including books or articles that enter our sphere of awareness.

Earlier I spoke about 'hidden director', but actually the one organizing the events in our lives is anyone but our True Self, we are, our divine part living outside space and time, who knows perfectly the reason we are here for.

The same way of a dream, time and space are only fake constructions created by our mind. Every event, past or future, exist simultaneously here and now based on our thoughts, beliefs or expectation we live correspondents events, meaning the materialization of our primary vibration.

Time does not exist and all of the books and articles that we will read, as much as the seminars and lessons we will attend, they already exist somewhere in space-time. They always existed.

But we know that there nothing and no one out there, that that space-time only exists in our mind and that we are the creators of any event, book, seminar we meet along our road. We put those there, on our path, long before coming to Earth, so that one day we could enjoy them.

Well, we are the creators of everything that could help our growth, creating an 'education program', which is the path of growth, and the 'didactic material', which is made of books, articles and seminars we are able to use.

Isn't it absurd? If we admit to be the only architect of our reality it cannot be more true, otherwise we would have to think of the existence of a hypothetical something or someone out there outside of us, but this would ruin the principle which says that we are the only architects of the world we experience, but above all it would violate the principle that says that we are one and one only with the Universe.

And maybe now it is clear why I claim that this book was written by you, and that you put that in your path of growth, so that you could read it at the right time.

We could end discussion here, but if you find pleasure in following me, I would like to talk to you about an even bigger concept that derives from what we said so far.

To say that space and time do not exist and that they are only illusions in our mind doesn't say so much about it, because probably none of you has a clear picture of what that means.

We all have direct experience of space and time. If we want to go to a distant place, indeed, we have to make it that far and it would take time to go there.

So where's the illusion?

Let's start from the conclusion: time and space exist only as a consequence of the fact that we don't know about our being divine and we don't recognize to be One a whole with the entire Universe.

Well, let's start from space. As you know for sure, we keep creating reality based on our most intimate beliefs. As such, until we believe to be separated one from another, we will necessarily create a world where things are separated by a space.

Physics, thanks to the quantic entanglement principle, it demonstrated that two particles, even if they are separated and placed at very far distances between each other, they always behave as the were one only particle. From the point of view of physics the, the space that apparently separates those particles does not exist.

Space is only our creation to justify our mistaken conviction that we are separated from the entire Universe.

What about time? We said that our true nature is not the body we live in, but rather our True Self, who is the divine being that lives outside space and time, that know the real Reality, not being influenced by the illusion of the apparent world we live in. Well, the fact that we don't believe to already know the real Reality, it makes us create a temporal separation between us and the hypothetical moment of our enlightenment. Actually we already are enlightened beings, we always have, but we don't believe it so we think that it takes time to reach that enlightenment.

Time is only our creation to justify our mistaken conviction that we are not enlightened beings who already know the real Reality.

This is why you wrote all of the books you are going to meet along the way, this one included, and you are reading some at the time, during your long journey of research, with the only purpose of remembering everything.

Printed in Great Britain
by Amazon